About the Author

Dhananjay Singh (Jay) is a post graduate in management, having more than 18 years of experience working in diversified SAP areas like S/4 HANA, SAP Fiori, SAP Hybris C4C and SAP Leonardo (IoT), S/4 HANA Finance, S/4 HANA Logistics, IS Oil and SAP Solution Manager.

Mr. Jay has 15 years of SAP experience with world's largest Enterprise Solution consulting companies like IBM Global Business Services (GBS), HCL Technologies and Hewlett Packard Enterprise. In his consulting career he has worked with several leading customers like Shell, SKF, Maersk Line, Friesland Campina, Exxon Mobil, Heineken, Dr. Pepper Snapple Group, National University of Singapore etc. in the capacity of Business Consultant, Business

Analyst, Implementation Consultant and Solution architect. His core areas of expertise are supply chain management, Cloud for customer, process design, ERP implementation and deployment of industry best practices. Lately his area of interest are S/4 HANA, SAP Hybris Customer for Cloud and SAP Leonardo along with digital transformation technology.

Preface

In last five years, SAP focus towards digital transformation brought CAMS (Cloud, analytics, Mobile, Social and Security) transformation to the fore. Our environment is changing, at an unprecedented pace in every aspect of daily life. It includes the way businesses operate, organizations need to digitize to succeed. To keep up with the pace of innovation S/4 HANA provides customers with a proven path toward the digital transformation they need. SAP S/4 HANA enables real-time business processes, predictive analysis, and simulation, and offers a state-of-the-art user experience and increased agility and efficiency.

SAP's guiding principle to manage this balance and control the changes required for the conversion to SAP S/4HANA. SAP release the simplification List time to time along with updated migration worklist and best practices document so that customers can prepare early in the planning phase. SAP releases/ update SAP Notes frequently so if you are referring this book please check the latest version of SAP Note mentioned during your migration.

From a technological perspective, I have never seen SAP system so open to adopt or integrate any new technology, everything now seems possible with SAP. Amongst all the changes that S/4HANA can bring, the one that most affect the SAP end-users is what they will see on their screens. It is not a nice-looking screen, but new services and concepts, analytical and real-time data, personalization at their fingerprints. We need to ensure that they feel comfortable to adopt the new technologies and processes changes coming up with S/4 HANA.

About this Book

This book introduces you to the tasks associated with the one step conversion and migration from ECC (any EHP) to S/4 HANA. This book is intended for SAP Functional Consultant, SAP S/4HANA application consultants, SAP Project Managers, SAP solutioning team members, IT managers, solution architects and SAP existing users. This book uses screenshots however pictures of SAP was avoided due to SAP copyright. The objective of this book is to provide insight into the SAP S/4HANA step by step migration process.

Acknowledgments

I'd like to take this opportunity to thank you SAP technology where I am employed for more than 15 years in 8 countries. I am grateful to my previous companies Hewlett Packard Enterprise and IBM GBS SAP Service Line who have provided me with the opportunities to work in emerging technologies.

My wife has been the prime mover and the source of strength all along to start the series "Learn SAP in 24 hours" collection. Any revenue earned from these books directly goes to Vivekananda Orphanage Ashram West Bengal and Auxilium Convent School Bandel to support orphan girl child education.

Structure and Content of this Book

The book starts with a short introduction of SAP S/4 HANA. In **Chapter 1** and **Chapter 2**, outlining the pre-requisites of one step migration to S/4 HANA from any ECC EHPx in general, technical and functional perspective in particular. You will learn the steps to be performed as a pre-requisite for S/4 HANA conversion.

Chapter 3 will explain the technical pre-checks and steps needed to be performed for the system conversion to SAP S/4 HANA 1610.

Chapter 4 will guide you the steps to be performed as a preparation, execution and post conversion activities. This is the most important chapter in this book and needs to be followed step by step during S/4 HANA system conversion.

Chapter 5 devoted to data conversion. Detailed technical and functional steps provided for master data and transactional data conversion.

Post conversion steps covered in **Chapter 6**. Here you will get the step by step process of post conversion customization.

Chapter 7 is the last chapter in this book and covers miscellaneous topics related to S/4 HANA conversion and Migration like productive hardware sizing, Maintenance planner check, glimpses of Fiori-end server, custom code optimization overview, using pre-configured mode and important OSS SAP Notes relevant for conversion.

All in all, you will see that this book provides you with a complete package in a comprehensive way, of all that you need to know, to successfully migrate to S/4 HANA system from any of EHP level of ECC.

1. Table of Contents

THIS PAGE INTENTIONALLY LEFT BLANK

1. Introduction

SAP S/4HANA introduced the next generation and latest evolution of SAP's core application platforms, with redesign and reengineering to maximize the in-memory capabilities of the SAP HANA database. Although SAP presents SAP S/4HANA as a new platform that introduces some radical changes to the architecture of the SAP system, it is not a different product which requires greenfield implementation. SAP S/4HANA builds on the well-proven functional base of the SAP Enterprise management and can be introduced in an evolutionary, gradual, and selective way into an existing SAP environment.

SAP S/4HANA is revolutionary in that it brings in transactional simplicity, advanced analytics, innovation, and enhancement of the functionality as compared to traditional SAP ERP. SAP S/4HANA provides a complete rewrite of SAP ERP code phased by functional area and moves some application code to the database layer as stored database procedures. It provides a new data model by removing old tables, aggregate tables, and index tables to create fewer columnar-based tables and deliver a real single version of the truth. SAP S/4HANA is designed with an SAP Fiori integrated user experience that provides users with instant insight and works on any mobile device. It offers real-time operational analytics on the SAP ERP platform, reducing the dependency on SAP Business Warehouse (SAP BW) reporting.

On the technical side, migration to SAP S/4HANA redefines data aggregation using the in-memory capabilities of the SAP HANA database. This allows for reduction of data footprint because calculations for transactions are performed on the database layer instead of the traditional application layer on an ad hoc basis.

Before moving to S/4 HANA, customers should plan their resources and educate their IT resources to bring them up to the required level, so that they can adopt early and assist business to adopt the changes. Business users are using ECC from decades and changing the processes established over decade will always be a challenge. Within company IT organization, IT people need subject knowledge to educate business, so business can adapt to new changes leaving their decade old comfort of SAP transactions. In a nutshell, using SAP provided tool DMO of SUM you can migrate directly ECC (any EHP) to S/4 HANA Enterprise Management. Strategic decisions on enabling S/4 HANA innovations will need change management through adoption, while traditional capabilities or SAP Business Suite on HANA will remain available as compatibility scope, and leave the extent of change management to be decided at the time of system conversion.

2. Prerequisites of S/4 HANA Conversion

2.1. S/4HANA Impact Assessment

Many impact assessment tools are available in the market which are easy to run and get the result of impact analysis. Few popular tools for impact analysis are Panaya, Smartshift, Winshuttle etc. I will explain briefly how you can do the impact analysis without using any 3rd party S/4HANA Conversion Assessment tool. S/4 HANA impact assessment helps customer to understand the impact of moving their SAP systems on anyDB to SAP S/4HANA. These are the steps you need to follow for impact assessment:

In your ECC System apply Note 2182725 (S4TC Delivery of the SAP S/4HANA System Conversion Checks). Remember to apply this note in client 000 and the report to be executed in client 000 only.

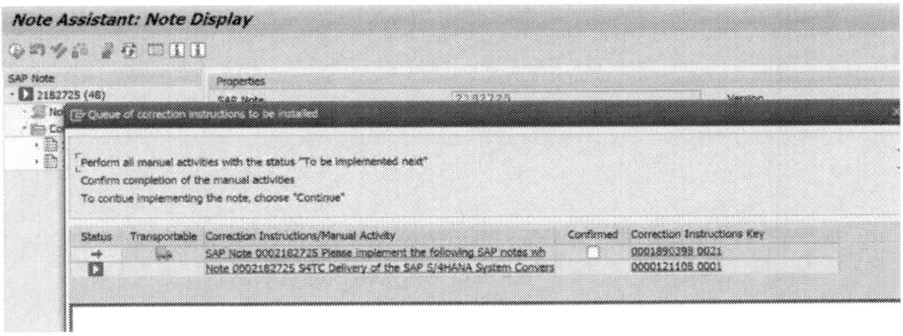
Note Assistant: Note Display
SAP Note
2182725 (46)
Properties
Queue of correction instructions to be installed
Perform all manual activities with the status "To be implemented next"
Confirm completion of the manual activities
To contiue implementing the note, choose "Continue"
Status
Transportable
Correction Instructions/Manual Activity
Confirmed
Correction Instructions Key
SAP Note 0002182725 Please implement the following SAP notes wh
0001890398 0021
Note 0002182725 S4TC Delivery of the SAP S/4HANA System Convers
0000121108 0001

SAP Note 2182725 requires, 21 SAP Notes to be downloaded and applied manually. Once all these notes are applied and confirmed in the dialog.

The dependent notes will appears after confirmation, it will show SAP Note 2185960 with approximately 36 dependent notes. These notes can be applied automatically so click (green tick box) and go.

2.2. Technical Prerequisites

There are number of requirements to enable conversion to SAP S/4HANA 1610. One of the pre-conversion activities is to analyze the current technical system details and landscape to ensure the conversion is possible.

2.2.1. Check Release

For a one-step migration conversion, the source system must be at a minimum release level:

- SAP ERP 6.0 including enhancement packages up to 8
- S/4HANA Finance add-on 1.0 for SAP Business Suite powered by SAP HANA
- S/4HANA Finance 1503
- S/4HANA 1511

2.2.2. Confirm Unicode Compliance

Unicode is a pre-requisite for conversion to S/4HANA. Check whether the system is already Unicode by going to the menu and navigating to System > Status sub-menus.

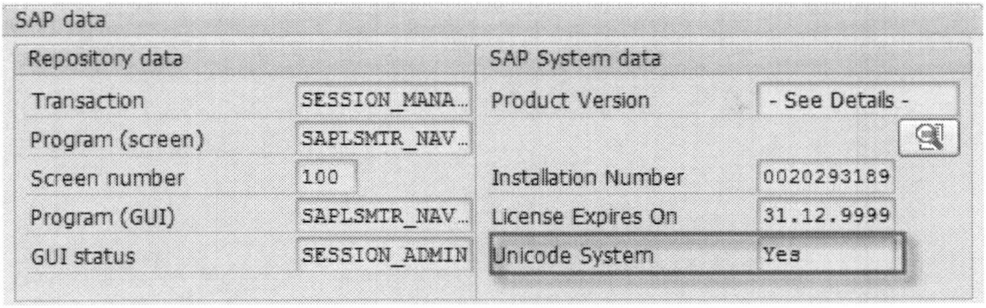
SAP data
Repository data
Transaction
SESSION_MANA...
Program (screen)
SAPLSMTR_NAV...
Screen number
100
Program (GUI)
SAPLSMTR_NAV...
GUI status
SESSION_ADMIN
SAP System data
Product Version
- See Details -
Installation Number
0020293189
License Expires On
31.12.9999
Unicode System
Yes

If you found non-Unicode then you need to perform Unicode conversion using the Software Provisioning Manager (SWPM). After that use the Database Migration Option (DMO) of SUM to combine the system update and database conversion as the second step in the conversion procedure (two-step).

2.2.3. Verify Single Stack

SAP ERP Java components are obsolete with SAP S/4HANA. Dual-stack systems (AS ABAP and AS Java combined in one system) are not supported for the conversion. The source system has to be an Application Server (AS) ABAP system only. You can confirm the current system setup using transaction SM51. If the system is a dual stack system, J2EE service will be shown in SM51.

Message Types
Status
Dialog Batch Update Upd2 Spool ICM J2EE
Active

If the system is a dual-stack system you need to split it prior to the conversion. Dual-stack split procedure is offered by Software Provisioning Manager 1.0 (integrated as of SL Toolset 1.0 SPS09; no longer offered standalone). Going further we will explain how to split dual stack system.

2.2.4. Check Oracle Source DB version

If using Oracle database as source database and DMO (Database Migration Option) for SUM (Software Update Manager) is used to perform a conversion to S/4HANA 1610 or any other product based on SAP NetWeaver 7.50 or higher version, ensure that Oracle DB version 12 or higher is used.

2.2.5. Check SAP ECC JAVA Instance

If using SAP ECC Java instance connected to the SAP ECC Server via the same product system in Solution Manager SMSY/LMDB and performing a conversion of the SAP ECC server to SAP S/4HANA 1610, you need to decouple the technical Java system containing the corresponding SAP ERP Java instance from the common product systems in SMSY/LMDB.

The following SAP ERP Java instances are not supported in the context of SAP S/4HANA 1610:

- SAP FSCM - Biller Direct
- SAP XECO
- SAP XECO - design time
- SAP XSS (Self Services)

- SAP XSS Core
- SAP Retail Store Applications
- SAP Utility Customer E-Service
- SAP Learning Sol-Frontend CP
- Portal Content
- Portal Content Common
- Portal Content Self Services
- SAP Integration for BCONS

2.2.6. Hardware and Software Requirements

Ensure the S/4HANA target system has the appropriate hardware (CPU, main memory, disk space, and swap space) by performing delta sizing. Read SAP Note 1872170 – Business Suite on HANA and S/4HANA sizing report to find the latest note to be applied through SNOTE. Run the report /SDF/HDB_SIZING in background. You can select the parameter as per requirement, if you have more processes available increase number of parallel processes.

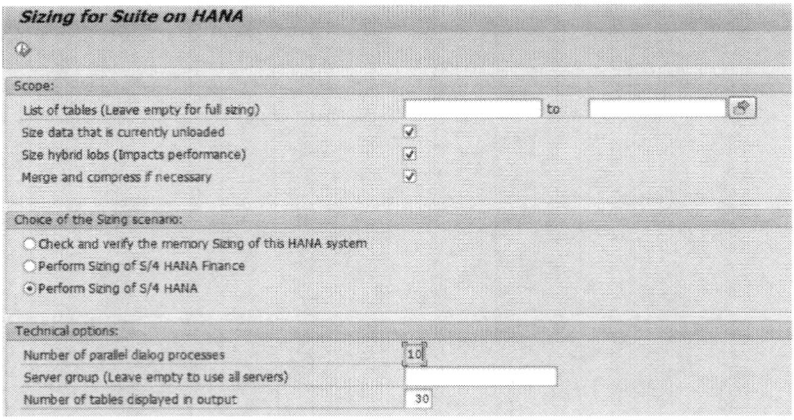
Sizing for Suite on HANA
Scope:
List of tables (Leave empty for full sizing)
to
Size data that is currently unloaded
Size hybrid lobs (Impacts performance)
Merge and compress if necessary
Choice of the Sizing scenario:
Check and verify the memory Sizing of this HANA system
Perform Sizing of S/4 HANA Finance
Perform Sizing of S/4 HANA
Technical options:
Number of parallel dialog processes
10
Server group (Leave empty to use all servers)
Number of tables displayed in output
30

The sizing report will provide you the indication whether system is Unicode and you can go for a single step migration. It also indicates Version of OS, version of Database, SAP Kernel and Netweaver Release. Based on the result of this report you can decide any additional memory requirement for a shadow instance.

2.2.7. SAP Fiori Front-End Server

As a prerequisite, the database of the central hub system has to be migrated to SAP HANA or SAP ASE that support S/4HANA 1610 front-end server if needed. It is possible to combine the upgrade of front-end server and the installation of SAP Fiori for S/4HANA 1610. The existing front-end server may be used for Fiori for S/4HANA 1610. However, if the NetWeaver version of front-end server is lower than 7.51, the front-end server must be upgraded to

NetWeaver 7.51 because SAP S/4HANA 1610 requires minimum of SAP NetWeaver 7.51 as front-end server.

2.2.8. Maintenance Planner

Setting up the Maintenance Planner tool is the first step in the conversion process. Using Maintenance Planner is mandatory for conversion to S/4HANA. The Maintenance Planner has replaced the Maintenance Optimizer, which is not supported by SAP S/4HANA. This step creates the download files (add-ons, packages, and stack configuration file – the input for SUM) that the Software Update Manager (SUM) uses to upgrade SAP S/4HANA 1610. The Maintenance Planner performs the following checks:

i. Checks for always-on and always-off business functions
ii. Supported Industry Solutions
iii. Supported Add-Ons

If there is no valid conversion path for any of the items listed above (for example, an add-on is not released for the conversion yet), the Maintenance Planner prevents the conversion. After the check, the Maintenance Planner creates the stack configuration file (stack.xml).

2.2.9. Custom Code Check

Before converting to S/4HANA, check existing custom code against the S/4HANA simplifications in a SAP NetWeaver 7.5 system. These simplifications are loaded into the Custom Code Check Tool. After execution, the tool returns a list of instances where existing custom code does not comply with the scope and data structure of SAP S/4HANA 1610, on premise edition. Below are the steps to run Custom Code Check Tool:

1. Run the report SYCM_DOWNLOAD_REPOSITORY_INFO as a job. The Custom Code Analyser detects all references to SAP objects in the custom code. As result of successful job execution, metadata for these references stored in a ZIP file. This job takes few hours to run so it should not be run in the production system. Recommended to refresh QAS system with PRD and then run the Custom Code Analyser.
2. Execute the report SYCM_DOWNLOAD_REPOSITORY_INFO, on the SYCM custom repository download page choose to download ZIP file icon to download of the ZIP file.
3. Execute the program SYCM_UPLOAD_REPOSITORY_INFO to import the Custom Code Analysis Result into the Evaluation System. This enable you to upload the Custom Code Worklist in the evaluation system.
4. By running the program SYCM_DISPLAY_SIMPLIFICATIONS, you will get the results

of the custom code analysis. The results provide you the objects that are impacted and the classification. The worklist provides Processing Status, Customer Object Type, Customer Object Name, Customer Subtype, Customer Subname/SAP Object Subname, Customer Package, Dependency Category and Application component,

5. More information for this tool is available on the SAP help Portal at http://help.sap.com/s4hana_op_1610.

ABAP team can carry out review of all existing custom code in above areas to ensure compatibility to the new data model.

2.3. Finance Functional Prerequisites

S/4HANA provides enhanced Finance functionality and the impact in the following areas should be considered early in the project:

- New General Ledger
- New Asset Accounting
- SAP Cash Management

You can do accounting Pre-checks following SAP Note 2333236 (Composite SAP Notes: Enhancements and message texts for the program RASFIN_MIGR_PRECHECK) along with accounting Components to SAP S/4HANA attached with SAP Note 2332030. To run the report RASFIN_MIGR_PRECHECK, apply SAP Note

1939592, it will access the requirement to migrating to new asset accounting.

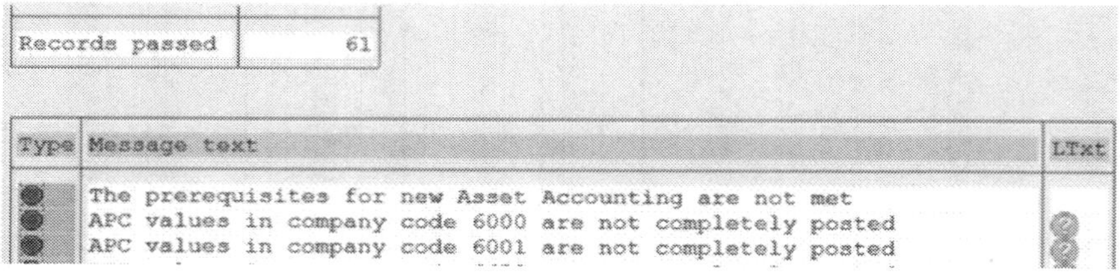

Records passed	61

Type	Message text		LTxt
●	The prerequisites for new Asset Accounting are not met		
●	APC values in company code 6000 are not completely posted		
●	APC values in company code 6001 are not completely posted		

Below are the different reports which need to run to access different area of Finance:

REPORT	PURPOSE
RFINDEX_NACC	Checks the consistency of the document views (BSIS, BSAS, BSID, BSAD, BSIK, and BSAK) with the line items in the BSEG table
RFINDEX_NACC	Checks the consistency of documents against transaction figures for all fiscal years not yet archived
SAPF190	Reconciles the classic General Ledger and the Accounts Receivable and Accounts Payable subledgers
TFC_COMPARE_VZ	Reconciles the new General Ledger and the Accounts Receivable and Accounts Payable subledgers
RAABST02RAABST01	Reconciles the General Ledger with Asset Accounting for the leading valuation and parallel valuation. Ref SAP Note 2390881.
RGUCOMP4	Compares ledgers with the new General Ledger
RM07MBST, RM07MMFI	Reconciles Materials Management (MM) with the General Ledger

2.3.1. General Ledger

S/4HANA provides support for multiple accounting principles using parallel ledgers and segmented financial statement reporting using document splitting – these processes are immediately supported post-conversion if the source system is already using the New General Ledger (New GL).

Conversion of Classic GL source systems is possible however New GL will need to be implemented in order to use document splitting functionality in S/4HANA 1610. If document splitting is required after conversion, then New GL should be implemented. If the functionality is not required, then conversion can be done from a Classic GL source system. As of release 1610, it is possible to implement parallel ledgers after converting to S/4HANA. SAP is working on document splitting conversion and it's expected to be includes with S/4HANA 1710 release.

2.3.2. Check Customization for S/4HANA Finance

Run the pre-check program RASFIN_MIGR_PRECHECK in all systems to validate that the ledger, company code and controlling area settings meet the required consistency for financial accounting conversion.

If any errors are identified, correct them before moving to the next conversion step.The pre-check program is included in SAP Note 2129306 that needs to be downloaded and installed. You will get a log of all components:

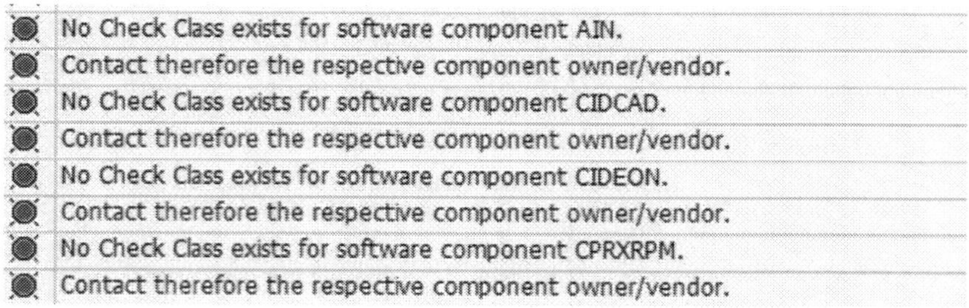
No Check Class exists for software component AIN.
Contact therefore the respective component owner/vendor.
No Check Class exists for software component CIDCAD.
Contact therefore the respective component owner/vendor.
No Check Class exists for software component CIDEON.
Contact therefore the respective component owner/vendor.
No Check Class exists for software component CPRXRPM.
Contact therefore the respective component owner/vendor.

2.3.3. New Asset Accounting

Asset Accounting is obsolete in S/4HANA 1610 and must be converted to New Asset Accounting. You need to activate the Financials Extension (EA-FIN) business function prior to system conversion. This is mandatory to be able to use the new posting functions provided by S/4HANA.

Note that in order to use EA-FIN, the following business functions are not allowed:

i. Lease Accounting Engine (LEA)
ii. Classic Real Estate Management (RE): You can use Flexible Real Estate Management (RE-FX) as an alternative.
iii. From Funds Management (PSM-FM) or Industry-Specific Component Public Sector (IS-PS): Requests with Reference to Asset

For details of these prerequisites and restrictions refer to SAP Note 2333236. The following customization activities of new Asset

Accounting must be performed in the system prior to actual conversion.

- Determine active charts of depreciation.
- Check accounting principle
- Check Ledger Group
- Assign accounting principle to ledger group
- Change definitions of depreciation areas
- Define transfer rules for the posting values of a depreciation area
- Specify transfer rules for depreciation terms of a depreciation area
- Parallel Currencies: Check Currency Type of Depreciation Area

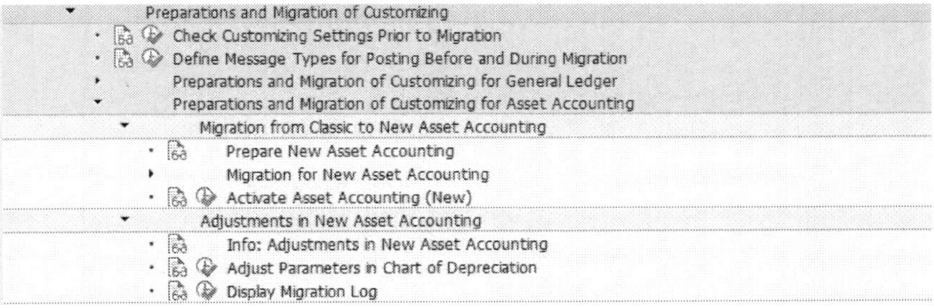
Preparations and Migration of Customizing
Check Customizing Settings Prior to Migration
Define Message Types for Posting Before and During Migration
Preparations and Migration of Customizing for General Ledger
Preparations and Migration of Customizing for Asset Accounting
Migration from Classic to New Asset Accounting
Prepare New Asset Accounting
Migration for New Asset Accounting
Activate Asset Accounting (New)
Adjustments in New Asset Accounting
Info: Adjustments in New Asset Accounting
Adjust Parameters in Chart of Depreciation
Display Migration Log

You need to perform the below customizations before migrating Asset Accounting data from ECC systems.

2.3.3.1. Define Ledger Group

Define ledger groups in this activity. The purpose and use for ledger groups is same as in the new GL concept of prior SAP releases, i.e. a ledger group is a combination of ledgers for the purpose of applying the functions and processes of General Ledger accounting to the group as a whole. The system uses the representative ledger of a ledger group to determine the posting period and to check whether the posting period is open.

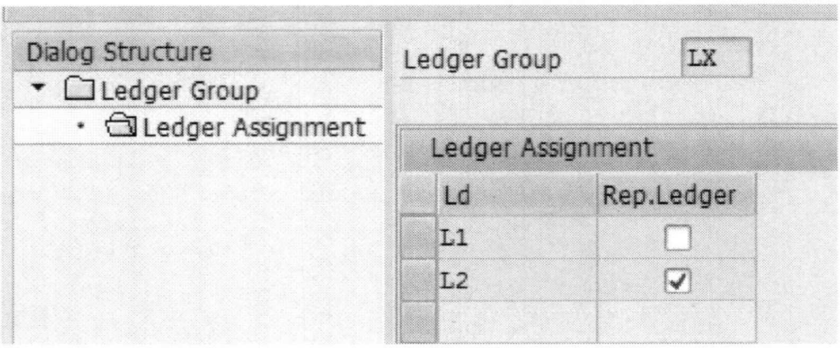
Dialog Structure
Ledger Group
Ledger Assignment
Ledger Group
LX
Ledger Assignment
Ld
Rep.Ledger
L1
L2

2.3.3.2. Assign Accounting Principle to Ledger Group

After the ledger groups are created, assign ledger groups to relevant accounting principles. You can find more details in SAP Note 1951069.

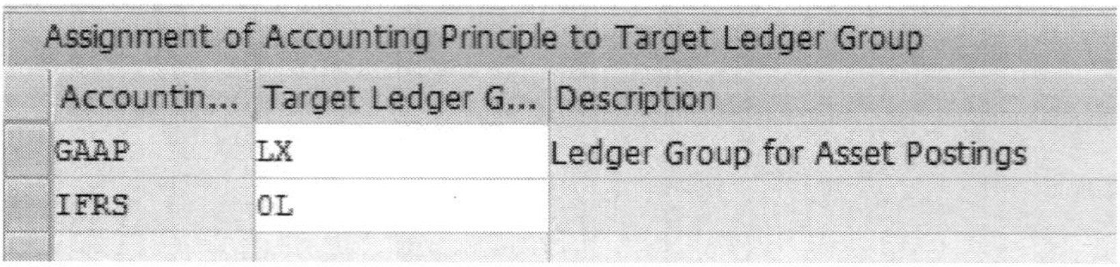

Assignment of Accounting Principle to Target Ledger Group

Accountin...	Target Ledger G...	Description
GAAP	LX	Ledger Group for Asset Postings
IFRS	0L	

2.3.3.3. Define Document Types for Posting in Controlling

Create new document types for postings in Controlling, e.g. for the manual reposting of primary costs. For documents types used in Controlling, the indicator G/L account must be set:

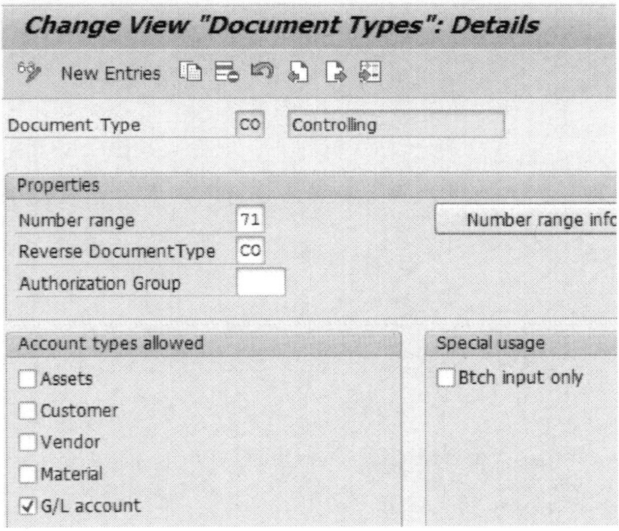

Change View "Document Types": Details

New Entries

| Document Type | CO | Controlling |

Properties

Number range	71	Number range infc
Reverse DocumentType	CO	
Authorization Group		

Account types allowed	Special usage
☐ Assets	☐ Btch input only
☐ Customer	
☐ Vendor	
☐ Material	
☑ G/L account	

2.3.3.4. Determine active charts of depreciation

Use transaction **OAOB** to assign productive Company Codes to the correct Chart of Depreciation and delete assignment for non-productive company codes:

CoCd	Company Name	Chrt dep	Description
1000	Company Code 1000	1000	Base Line Chart of depreciation
1010	Company Code 1010	1000	Base Line Chart of depreciation

Delete all links between sample charts of depreciation and Company Codes as they trigger an error during new Asset Accounting activation:

CoCd	Company Name	Chrt dep	Description
0001	SAP A.G.	0DE	Sample chart of depreciation: Germany
0003	SAP US (IS-HT-SW)	0DE	Sample chart of depreciation: Germany

2.3.3.5. Change definitions of depreciation areas

It is possible to automatically migrate the chart of depreciation using the automated conversion facility provided, we recommend to perform this pre-conversion activity manually as it offers flexibility and greater control over the eventual settings. In the automated process, the system performs the following

- Creates a ledger group for each leading depreciation area of a non-leading accounting principle. This ledger group will always be assigned to the leading ledger 0L.
- Assigns a name to the automatically created ledger group with the naming convention "&" +number of depreciation area+" &".

Additionally, before performing this asset accounting configuration, ensure all ledger groups created are assigned to their respective accounting principles. This applies regardless of the parallel accounting approach chosen i.e. ledger approach or accounts approach.

Chart of dep. 1000 Base Line Chart of depreciation

Define Depreciation Areas

Ar.	Name of depreciation area	Real	Trgt Group	Acc.Princ.	G/L
1	Book depreciation in local currency	✓	0L	IFRS	1 Area Posts in Realtime
10	Federal Tax ACRS/MACRS	✓	0L	IFRS	0 Area Does Not Post
11	Alternative Minimum Tax	✓	0L	IFRS	0 Area Does Not Post
12	Adjusted Current Earnings	✓	0L	IFRS	0 Area Does Not Post
13	Corporate Earnings & Profits	✓	0L	IFRS	0 Area Does Not Post

As shown above, assign each depreciation to an accounting principle, as dictated by business requirements. Crucially, only the leading depreciation area of each accounting principle is set to post Acquisition and Production Costs (APC) to the GL in real-time.

2.3.3.6. Specify Transfer of APC Values

In this step (transaction **OABC),** define transfer rules for the posting values of depreciation areas. In the *ValAd* field, adapt the value take-over such that the parallel depreciation areas adopt acquisition and production costs (APC) values of the leading depreciation areas (areas posting in real-time).

Note: The leading depreciation areas must never use values from a different depreciation area, and only depreciation areas using the same accounting principle can inherit values from each other, as shown in the figure below.

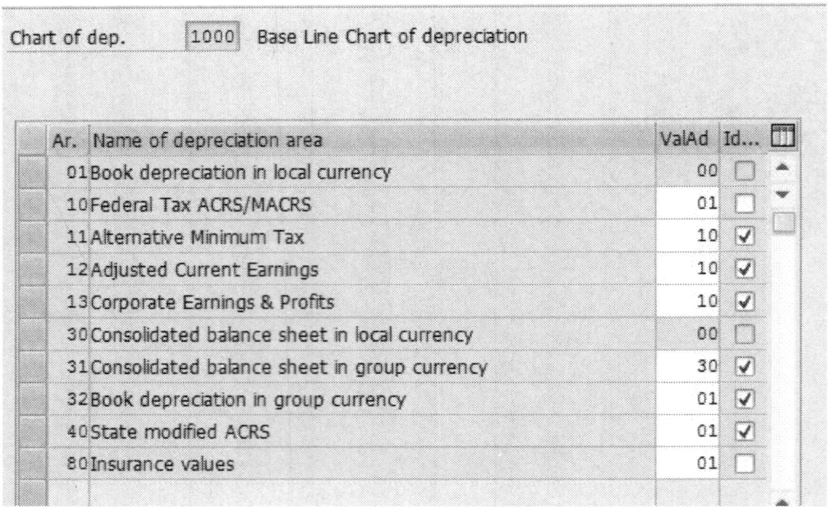
Chart of dep. 1000 Base Line Chart of depreciation

Ar.	Name of depreciation area	ValAd	Id...
01	Book depreciation in local currency	00	☐
10	Federal Tax ACRS/MACRS	01	☐
11	Alternative Minimum Tax	10	☑
12	Adjusted Current Earnings	10	☑
13	Corporate Earnings & Profits	10	☑
30	Consolidated balance sheet in local currency	00	☐
31	Consolidated balance sheet in group currency	30	☑
32	Book depreciation in group currency	01	☑
40	State modified ACRS	01	☑
80	Insurance values	01	☐

2.3.3.7. Specify Transfer of Depreciation Terms

Similar to APC values transfer, specify the depreciation area from which the depreciation terms are adopted by the current depreciation area. Except for the depreciation managing APC costs (leading area), the remaining depreciation areas can adopt values from the leading areas or each other, regardless of whether that area has a key that is greater or smaller than its own key.

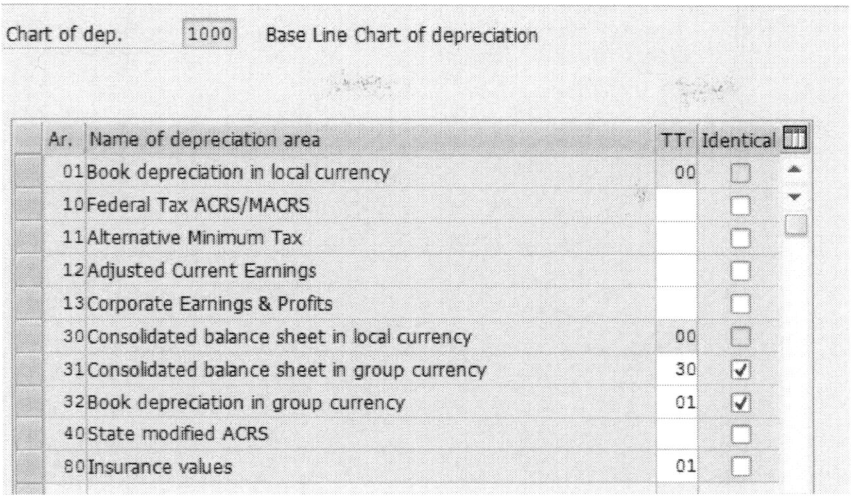

Chart of dep. 1000 Base Line Chart of depreciation

Ar.	Name of depreciation area	TTr	Identical
01	Book depreciation in local currency	00	☐
10	Federal Tax ACRS/MACRS		☐
11	Alternative Minimum Tax		☐
12	Adjusted Current Earnings		☐
13	Corporate Earnings & Profits		☐
30	Consolidated balance sheet in local currency	00	☐
31	Consolidated balance sheet in group currency	30	☑
32	Book depreciation in group currency	01	☑
40	State modified ACRS		☐
80	Insurance values	01	☐

2.3.3.8. Define Asset Balance Sheet Accounts of Parallel Valuation as Reconciliation Accounts

If migrating from a Classic Asset Accounting system that uses the accounts approach to parallel accounting (either New or Classic GL system), define the Asset Balance Sheet accounts of parallel valuation as reconciliation accounts. Do this in the "Preparation for Going live" menu of the Asset accounting customizing screen instead of individually in the GL Account maintenance screen.

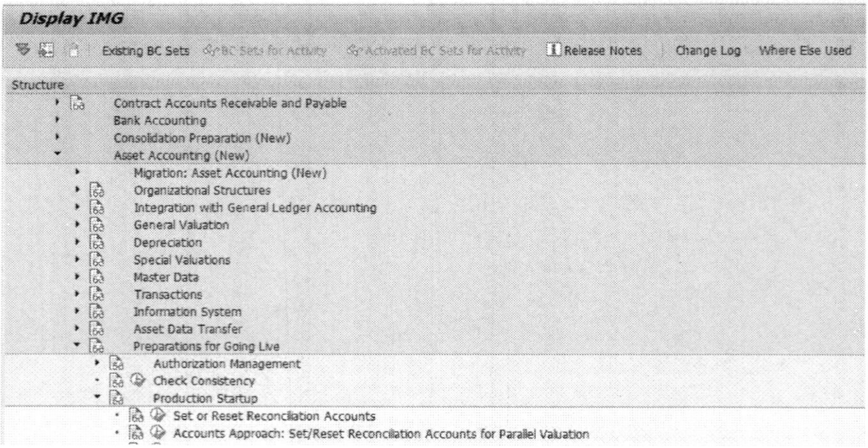
Display IMG
Existing BC Sets
Release Notes
Change Log
Where Else Used
Structure
Contract Accounts Receivable and Payable
Bank Accounting
Consolidation Preparation (New)
Asset Accounting (New)
Migration: Asset Accounting (New)
Organizational Structures
Integration with General Ledger Accounting
General Valuation
Depreciation
Special Valuations
Master Data
Transactions
Information System
Asset Data Transfer
Preparations for Going Live
Authorization Management
Check Consistency
Production Startup
Set or Reset Reconciliation Accounts
Accounts Approach: Set/Reset Reconciliation Accounts for Parallel Valuation

Click the "Set Reconciliation Ind. For All Accounts button" to activate for all applicable reconciliation accounts.

2.3.3.9. Define Technical Clearing Account for Integrated Asset Acquisition

Define a technical clearing account for integrated asset acquisitions. For an integrated asset acquisition posting, the system divides the business transaction into an operational part and a valuating part. For the operational part (vendor invoice), the system posts a document valid for all accounting principles against the technical clearing account for integrated asset acquisitions.

For each valuating part (asset posting with capitalization of the asset), the system generates ledger specific documents for all active ledgers, with the offsetting entry clearing against the technical clearing account for integrated asset acquisitions.

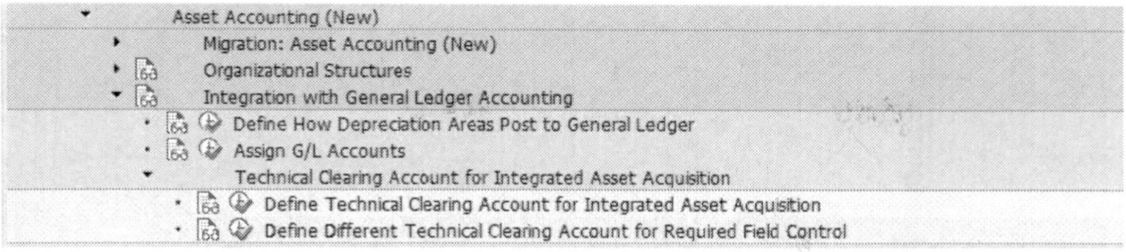
Asset Accounting (New)
Migration: Asset Accounting (New)
Organizational Structures
Integration with General Ledger Accounting
Define How Depreciation Areas Post to General Ledger
Assign G/L Accounts
Technical Clearing Account for Integrated Asset Acquisition
Define Technical Clearing Account for Integrated Asset Acquisition
Define Different Technical Clearing Account for Required Field Control

Use a balance sheet account created as a reconciliation account for fixed asset accounts but not set as line item managed.

2.3.3.10. Check Transaction Types

With the introduction of ledger specific posting functionality, ledger specific transaction types are no longer necessary in new asset accounting and must be deactivated. Make these transactions obsolete by checking the relevant box in the maintain view for transaction types as shown in the figure below. You should not delete these transaction types since they may have been used by previous transactions and removing them could result in inconsistencies in the system.

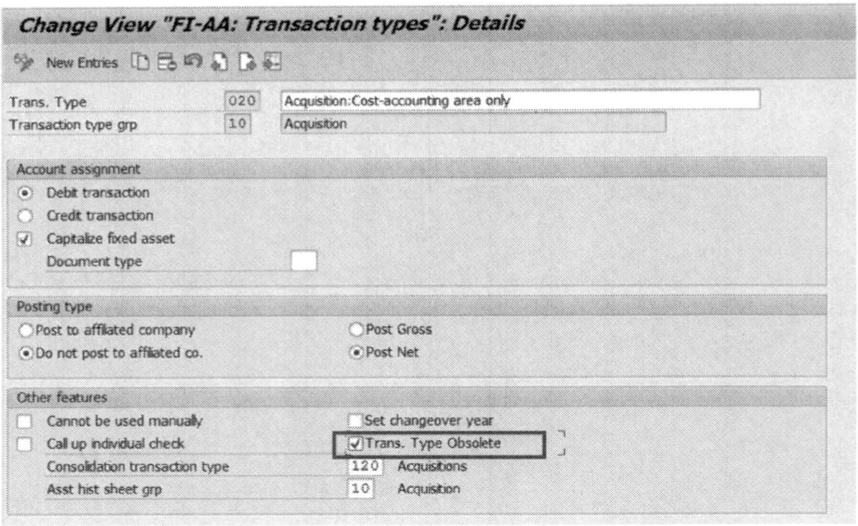
Change View "FI-AA: Transaction types": Details
New Entries
Trans. Type
020
Acquisition:Cost-accounting area only
Transaction type grp
10
Acquisition
Account assignment
Debit transaction
Credit transaction
Capitalize fixed asset
Document type
Posting type
Post to affiliated company
Do not post to affiliated co.
Post Gross
Post Net
Other features
Cannot be used manually
Call up individual check
Consolidation transaction type
Asst hist sheet grp
Set changeover year
Trans. Type Obsolete
120
Acquisitions
10
Acquisition

Transaction types for investment support or revaluation are exempt from the above and can continue to be restricted to depreciation areas. These transaction types are automatically generated by the system when a corresponding investment measure is created.

2.3.3.11. Check Prerequisites for Activation of New Asset Accounting

Execute pre-check program **RASFIN_MIGR_PRECHECK** in all production clients to validate prerequisites are met for conversion to new Asset Accounting. All errors encountered should be remediated before proceeding to the next conversion step.

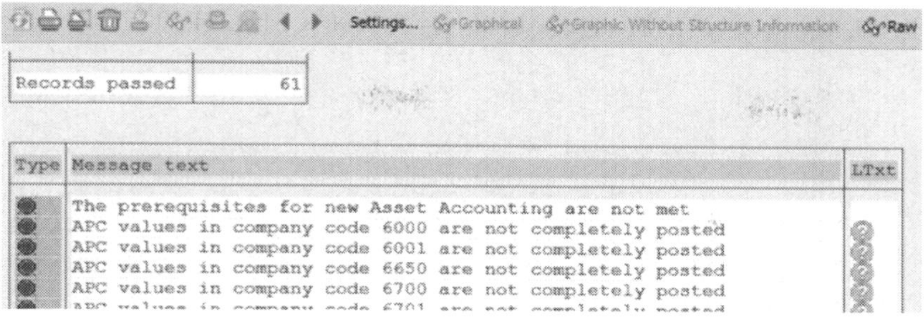
Settings...
Graphical
Graphic Without Structure Information
Raw
Records passed
61
Type
Message text
LTxt
The prerequisites for new Asset Accounting are not met
APC values in company code 6000 are not completely posted
APC values in company code 6001 are not completely posted
APC values in company code 6650 are not completely posted
APC values in company code 6700 are not completely posted

2.3.4. SAP Cash Management

Cash Management functions of Bank Account Management (BAM), Cash Operations and Liquidity Management are only available on S/4HANA via SAP Cash Management. The classic Cash and Liquidity Management (Cash Management and Liquidity Planner) function is no longer supported. **You can refer SAP Note** 2243327 for more details of prerequisites of cash management.

2.4. Logistics Functional Prerequisites

To migrate to S/4HANA, the prerequisites for Logistics listed in this section must be met before conversion.

2.4.1. SD Component Prerequisites

Before starting the conversion activities, the following main prerequisites should be addressed:

2.4.1.1. SD Credit Management

Transition to SAP Credit Management is mandatory with conversion to S/4HANA. Traditional Credit Management (FI-AR-CR) is not available in SAP S/4HANA on-premise edition 1610. It has been replaced by SAP Credit Management (FIN-FSCM-CR) for Financials and Sales and Distribution (SD). If using FI-AR-CR Credit Management, perform the steps outlined in Data Conversion to migrate the data to SAP Credit Management (FIN-FSCM-CR).

2.4.1.2. SD Revenue Recognition

In SAP S/4HANA, traditional SD Revenue Recognition is no longer available and has been replaced by SAP Revenue Accounting and Reporting functionality (RAR). If SD Revenue Recognition is currently implemented, evaluate whether a migration to SAP Revenue Accounting and Reporting is functionally possible before deciding to convert to the new system.

The new functionality supports the new revenue accounting standard as outlined in IFRS15 and adapted by local GAAPs. Prior to the conversion, migrate all sales order and contracts processed by SD Revenue Recognition to SAP RAR that:

i. are not fully delivered and invoiced
ii. have deferred revenue still to be realized
iii. have expected follow-on activities like quantity increase, credit memo or invoice cancellation

You can get more details in SAP Note 2267342 which updated time to time.

2.4.1.3. SD Foreign Trade

In SAP S/4HANA, SD Foreign Trade is no longer available and has been replaced by SAP Global Trade Services (GTS). If SD Foreign Trade is implemented, check whether third-party foreign trade systems are currently integrated and may therefore need to be adjusted by the respective third-party solution/service provider.
SAP GTS however can be connected on an additional instance to SAP S/4HANA to run the respective foreign trade processes. You can get more details in SAP Note 2267310 which updated time to time.

2.4.1.4. SD Contract Billing

Contract Billing is not available in SAP S/4HANA on-premise edition 1610. If Contract Billing is being used in the existing SAP ERP, then the business processes must be remodeled.

2.4.1.5. SD – FI/CA Integration with Distributed Systems

The integration between Contract Accounts Receivable and Payable (FI-CA) and Sales and Distribution (SD), when using each component in separate systems, is not yet available in SAP S/4HANA. The FI-CA within SAP S/4HANA on-premise, however, can be used as before.

As a prerequisite to conversion, ensure the Business Function LOG_SD_FICA_DISTRIBUTED is deactivated, since the system conversion to SAP S/4HANA is blocked when it is activated. The affected business processes also have to be remodeled if the conversion is to go ahead.

2.4.2. MM Component Prerequisites

The limitations related to the Logistics functionality listed below should be addressed prior to initiating the conversion:

i. Long Material Number implemented with Discrete Industries and Mill Products (DIMP)

ii. Production Planning Bill of Materials

iii. Planning at storage Location level now uses MRP Areas

2.4.2.1. Material Number Extension

With Discrete Industries and Mill Products (DIMP) installation where Long Material Number has already been activated, special consideration to the contents of the database field is required. You can refer SAP Note 2381633 for more updated details.

In all cases, execute the pre-check program MFLE_CLS4H_CHECKS_CC for the material number extension prior to conversion. Run the program in all clients that are used productively and in the background mode as execution times can be very long.

The program does not change the data in the system. It analyzes the tables to make sure that all framework data is converted to the new structure including customer-defined tables, fields and BOR types.

The check program is delivered with SAP Note 2216958. If you don't have this program in your ECC system, you need to apply this note in ECC system.

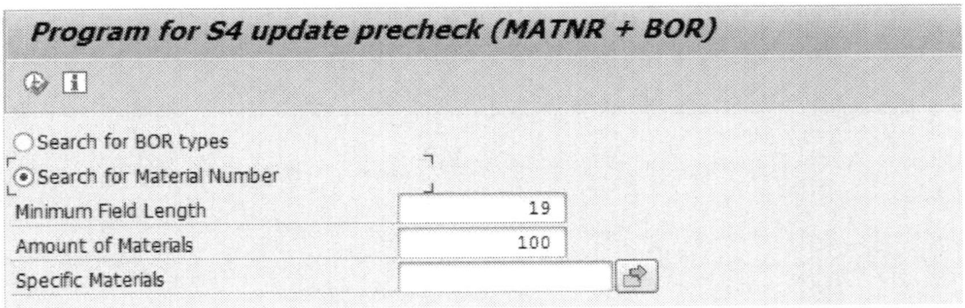
Program for S4 update precheck (MATNR + BOR)
Search for BOR types
Search for Material Number
Minimum Field Length
19
Amount of Materials
100
Specific Materials

2.4.2.2. Production Planning Bill of Material

Upgrading existing Bill of Material (BOM) requires maintenance of valid production versions. Execute program **CS_BOM_PRODVER_MIGRATION** to create production versions.

Valid production versions are required to allow BOM explosion in S/4HANA. The conversion of data for existing BOM selection methods like

(a) order quantity,

(b) explosion date,

(c) production version

All above production version need to merge into a production version approach. Executing the migration program makes merging all such data and associating it to a new/existing production version possible. For updated information refer SAP Note 2267880 and the BOM Migration program refer SAP Note 2194785

2.4.2.3. Run check program for Storage Location MRP

Release S/4HANA 1610 MRP uses simplified functionality where planning is done in one of the three MRP Areas:

i. Plant MRP Area

ii. MRP Area for Storage Locations

iii. MRP Area for Subcontractors

Storage Location MRP Area allows planning Storage Locations separately or excluding them from the run. More updated information available on SAP Note 2268045 so refer the current version of SAP Note.

Prior to conversion, execute the pre-check program MRP_AREA_STORAGE_LOC_MIGRATION to detect if storage location MRP is use in the source ERP. The program raises an error if planning on storage location level is detected. The program checks some prerequisites like MRP types, lot-sizing procedures, and MRP areas in customizing. If the required customizing entries are missing, they have to be manually created.

After the system conversion, run report PPH_SETUP_MRPRECORDS to populate the new planning file table with operative MRP records (PP-MRP) and the report PPH_SETUP_MRPRECORDS_SIMU for simulative MRP records (PP-MP-LTP).

The pre-check program is available in the SAP Note 2216528.

2.4.2.4. SAP Supplier Relationship Management (SRM)

The Supply Resource Management (SRM) module cannot be installed in the same system as S/4HANA. The processes will need to be re-implemented in SAP S/4HANA, therefore a careful evaluation needs to take place to ensure the new functionality meets requirements. Technical details of compatibility of SRM with S/4 HANA provided in SAP Note 2271166.

2.4.3. Other Logistics Components

It is important to consider logistics components that are not being supported by S/4HANA, including:

i. Commodity Management Sales and Procurement
ii. Environmental Health and Safety (EHS) functionality e.g., Industrial Hygiene and Safety (EHS-IHS), Occupational Health (EHS-HEA) etc.
iii. Product Lifecycle Management (PLM) e.g. Product Assembly, Product Designer Workbench, Access Control Management, The CAD Integration in SAP PLM, Recipe Management

2.5. Business Partner Approach

One significant change in S/4HANA is the transition from Customer/Vendor/Employee Master Data to Business Partners using the Customer Vendor Integration (CVI) to eliminate the redundancy of information in master data. This requirement must be reviewed carefully in the conversion process as it has impact across business processes in Financials, Logistics and Human Resources.

The central mechanism for managing master data for business partners, customers, and vendors in S/4HANA is the Business Partner approach. A prerequisite for conversion into the new system is that all Customers, Vendors, Employees and even existing Business Partners must first be converted into business partner.

Activate the customer/vendor transformation process as described below for the system to transfer all required fields into the business partner. The entire Business Partner data transfer including conversion and Business Partner post processing activities usually takes place in four phases illustrated in the following diagram.

Preparation
Synchronization
Conversion Process
Post Processing

2.5.1. Preparation for Business Partner Conversion

Perform the following customizing settings and activations.

i. Activate Business Function CA_BP_SOA:

If the Business Function CA_BP_SOA does not yet exist in the system, you need to create a new Business Function in the customer namespace with the switches VENDOR_SFWS_SC1 and VENDOR_SFWS_SC2. The new customer specific Business Function must be of type Enterprise Business Function (G).

ii. Check CVI customizing and make necessary changes

Check customizing settings with report **CVI_FS_CHECK_CUSTOMIZING** (implement note 1623677 as pre-requisite). Although any issues found are not necessarily fatal to conversion, correct them in customizing before proceeding further.

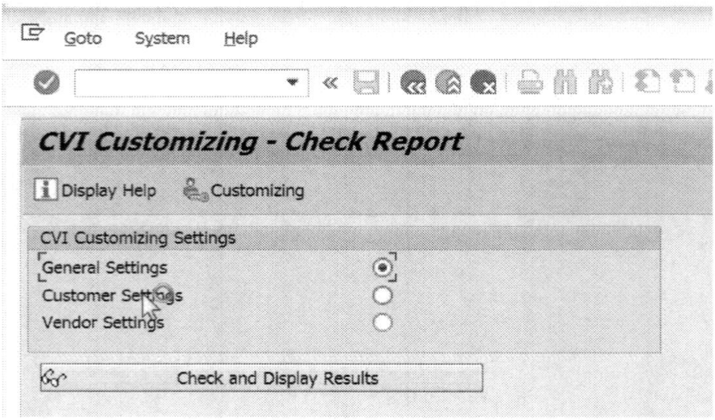
Goto
System
Help
CVI Customizing - Check Report
Display Help
Customizing
CVI Customizing Settings
General Settings
Customer Settings
Vendor Settings
Check and Display Results

Results of the check report are shown in the figures below.

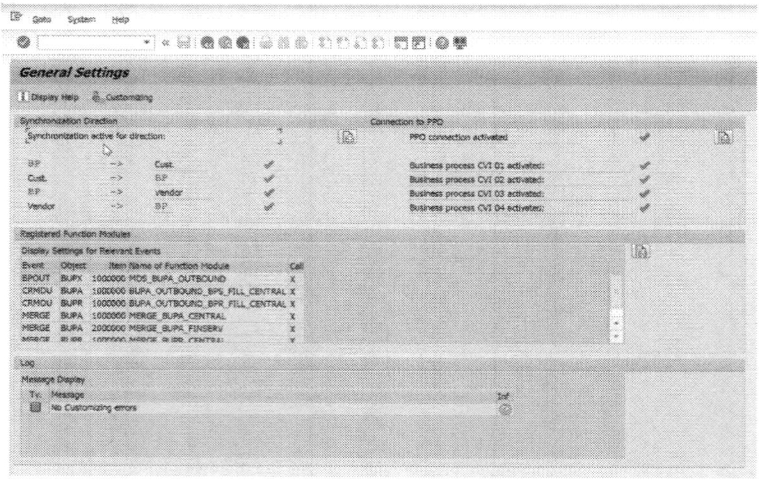
General Settings

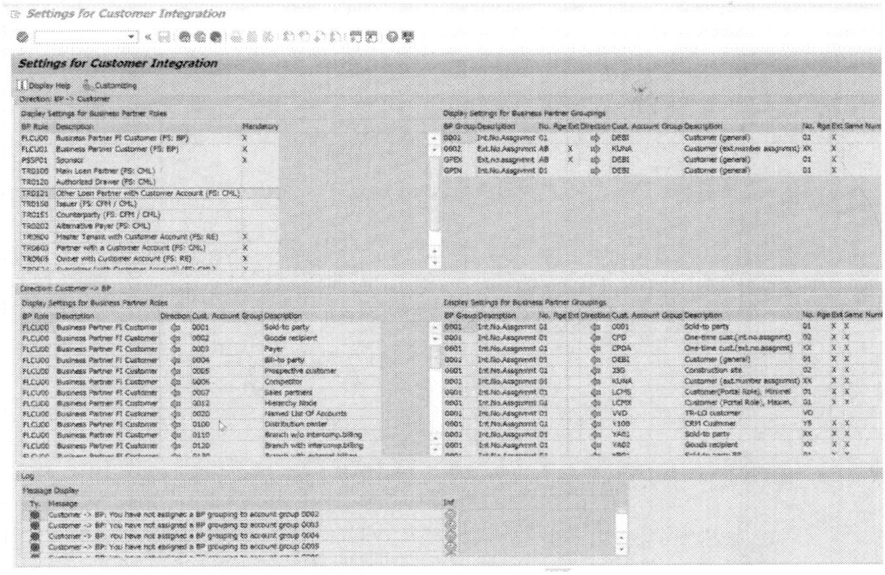
Settings for Customer Integration
Settings for Customer Integration

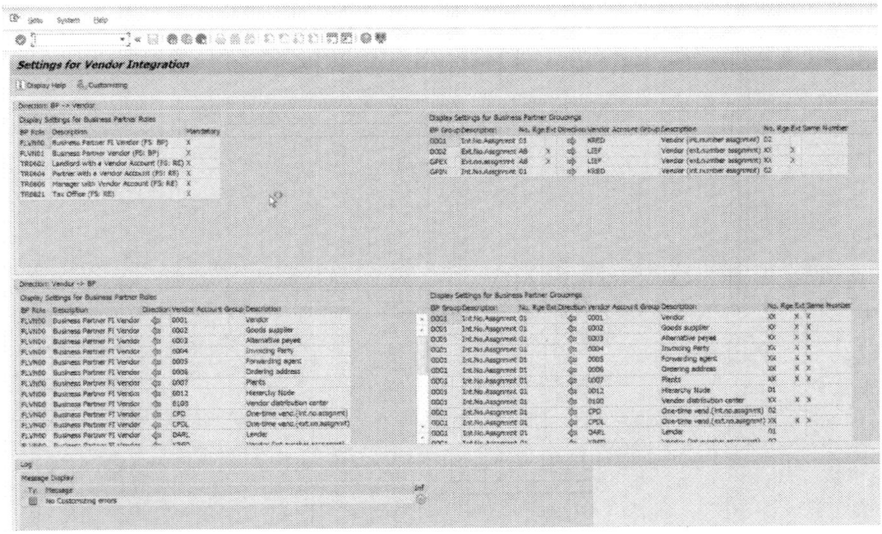
Settings for Vendor Integration

iii. Check and maintain BP customizing e.g. missing tax types.

Perform the following customizing activities needed for the conversion to BP under the IMG path Cross-Application Components > Master Data Synchronization:

iv. Activate Synchronization between Customer/Vendor and BP

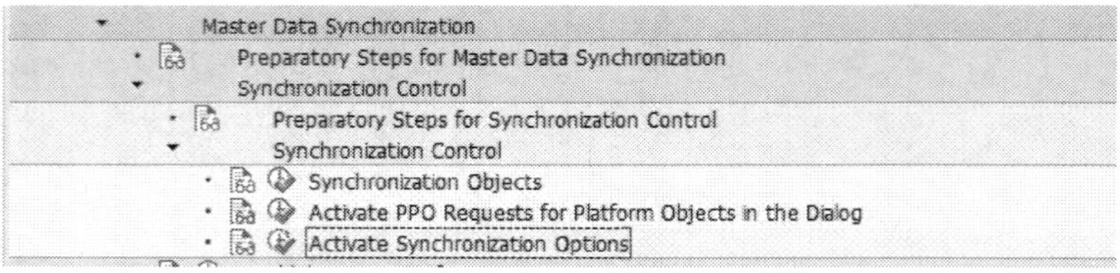
Master Data Synchronization
Preparatory Steps for Master Data Synchronization
Synchronization Control
Preparatory Steps for Synchronization Control
Synchronization Control
Synchronization Objects
Activate PPO Requests for Platform Objects in the Dialog
Activate Synchronization Options

v. Activate PPO Requests for Platform Objects in the Dialog

Connect the master data synchronization between the business partner and the customer/vendor to the Post Processing Office. The system uses this to write post-processing orders (PPO order) during the synchronization if an error occurs (investigated using transaction MDS_PPO2).

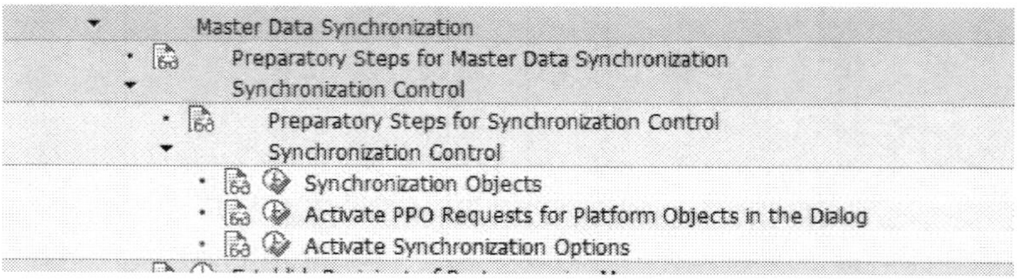
Master Data Synchronization
Preparatory Steps for Master Data Synchronization
Synchronization Control
Preparatory Steps for Synchronization Control
Synchronization Control
Synchronization Objects
Activate PPO Requests for Platform Objects in the Dialog
Activate Synchronization Options

If the PPO for the master data synchronization between the business partner and the customer/vendor is not activated, the system generates a dump in the synchronization if an error occurs. PPO entries or dumps are often caused by required entry fields that have not been adjusted. You can refer SAP Note 928616 ("BP_CVI: Customize of required entry fields at BP/cust/vendor") to resolve any error encountered.

vi. Activate Creation of Post-Processing Orders

In IMG cross-application functions, General Application Functions, assign CVI_01, CVI_02, CVI_03, CVI_04 to Component AP-MD and activate.

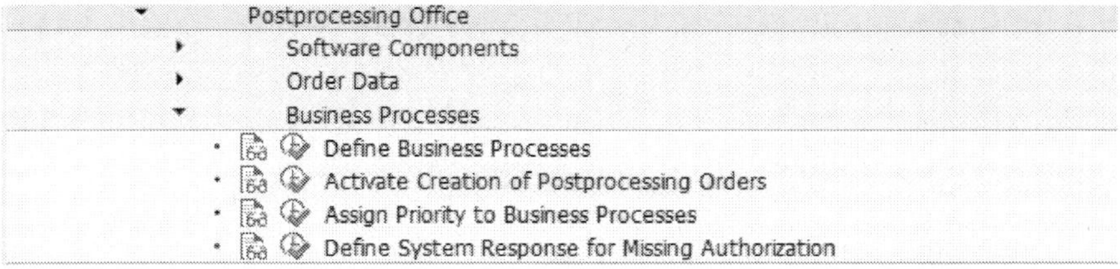
Postprocessing Office
Software Components
Order Data
Business Processes
Define Business Processes
Activate Creation of Postprocessing Orders
Assign Priority to Business Processes
Define System Response for Missing Authorization

vii. Customer/Vendor Integrations

For the synchronization from the Business Partner to Customer / Vendor, define the Customer/Vendor business partner role categories for Direction BP to Customer/Vendor.

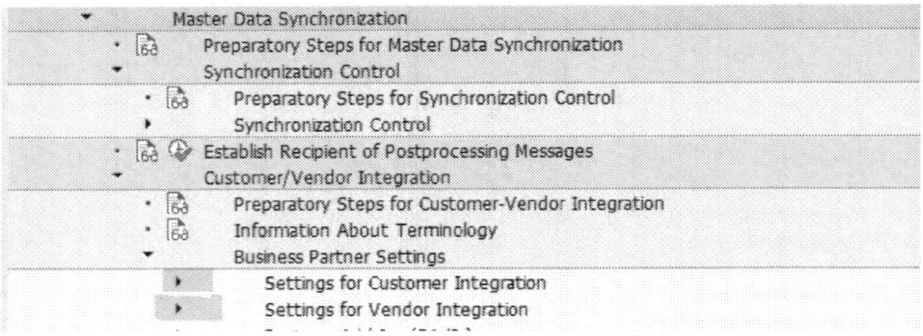
Master Data Synchronization
Preparatory Steps for Master Data Synchronization
Synchronization Control
Preparatory Steps for Synchronization Control
Synchronization Control
Establish Recipient of Postprocessing Messages
Customer/Vendor Integration
Preparatory Steps for Customer-Vendor Integration
Information About Terminology
Business Partner Settings
Settings for Customer Integration
Settings for Vendor Integration

viii. Prepare Mapping Tables for the BP Conversion

Execute the program **PRECHECK_UPGRADATION_REPORT** (referring SAP Note 2211312) to determine the mapping entries that are missing between CVI data and BP data. The report carries out the checks listed in the figure below.

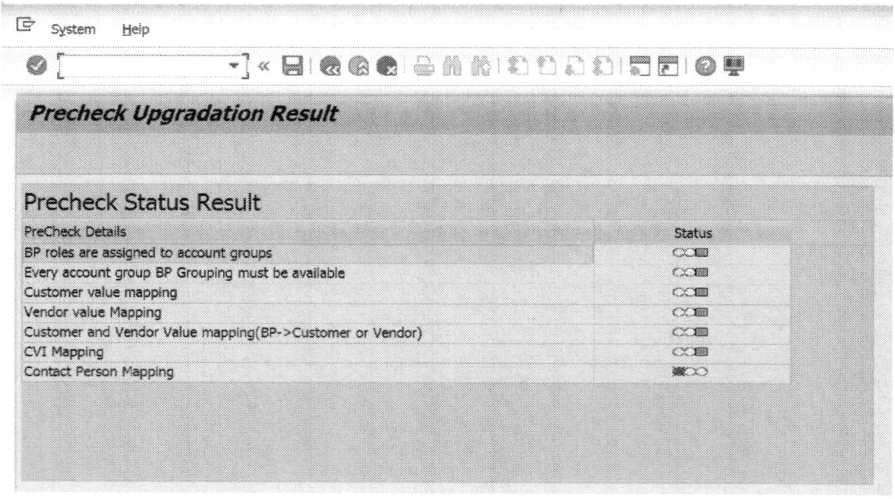
System
Help
Precheck Upgradation Result
Precheck Status Result
PreCheck Details
Status
BP roles are assigned to account groups
Every account group BP Grouping must be available
Customer value mapping
Vendor value Mapping
Customer and Vendor Value mapping(BP->Customer or Vendor)
CVI Mapping
Contact Person Mapping

Any missing mappings highlighted by the pre-check upgrade report can be fixed by making necessary configuration updates.

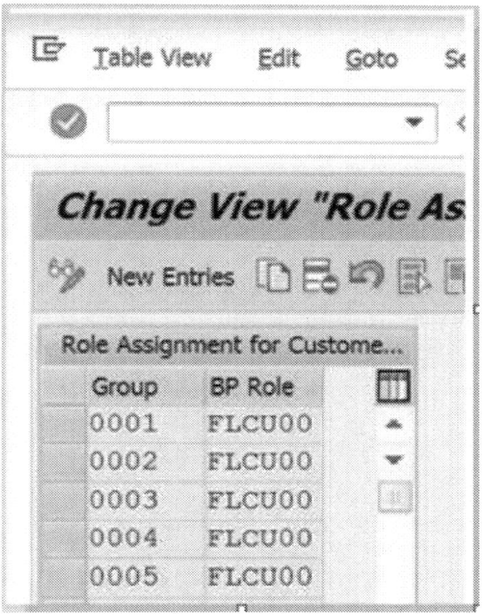
Table View
Edit
Goto
Change View "Role As
New Entries
Role Assignment for Custome...
Group
BP Role
0001
FLCU00
0002
FLCU00
0003
FLCU00
0004
FLCU00
0005
FLCU00

ix. Data Cleanup and Normalization:

Check and clean-up customer/vendor data.

2.5.2. Synchronization

Data load synchronization can be performed using Synchronization Cockpit. In case of an error during the synchronization process due to data/customizing mismatch the errors will be found in the monitor tab button "Call PPO in Synchronization Cockpit".

If required, run Business Partner Pre-Check **PRECHECK_UPGRADATION_REPORT** to verify the results accordingly and match the results as mentioned in SAP Note 2211312.

The customer/vendor transformation is bidirectional. It is possible to both process customer/vendor master records from business partner maintenance as well as populate data from customer/vendor processing to the business partner. After the successful S/4 conversion process; activate the post processing for direction Business Partner.

2.6. Country Versions

Check the country release information and restrictions detailed in SAP Note 2349004 to ensure there is no specific localization considerations resulting from conversion to S/4HANA.

The following localization release information exist:

i. Available languages: SAP Note 2380938.
ii. CEEISUT Retrofit: Business Functions. See SAP Notes 2323221 and 1014997
iii. CEEISUT Retrofit: Business Functions - Modifying Assignments for CEEISUT 600. See SAP Note 2330962.
iv. Brazil: Reporting. See SAP Note 2195701.
v. Japan: Retrofit of Expiration Date Management (EDM) and Choai Route Management. See SAP Note 2383164

vi. Israel: Annexing Solution. See SAP Note 2298073.

vii. S/4HANA Oil & Gas for Brazil: GLP (Gás liquefeito de petróleo) is not supported with S/4HANA 1610 and subsequent releases

viii. Greece: Due to the complexity and variability of the controlling setup for production companies

ix. Japan: Subcontracting (SCC). See SAP Note 2349063

x. Address Management for Turkey (IS-U). See SAP Note 2349019

xi. EC Sales & Purchase List Hungary on SRF. See SAP Note 2353686

xii. Availability of Statutory Reporting Framework (SRF): See SAP Note 2380053

xiii. Some apps with language restrictions. See SAP Note 2387302.

3. Preparation for System Conversion to SAP S/4HANA 1610

3.1. Perform Pre-Checks

The pre-checks are required to ensure the source system is compatible with the conversion process. The program checks for consistent "Check Class" definitions for all components prior to conversion. Any issues found must then be remediated by opening an SAP ticket or contacting your implementation partner. The checking program also verifies the readiness of the source system for upgrade by the Software Update Manager (SUM). The system validates the implemented components including:

i. Global Trade (EA-GLTRADE)
ii. Financial Services (EA-FINSERV)
iii. FI and CO Component Configuration settings
iv. SD Credit Management
v. SD Revenue Recognition
vi. ARIBA Business Services Add-On
vii. SD data model
viii. MM data model
ix. Retail (EA-Retail)
x. ECC-Discrete Industries & Mill Products (DIMP) Master.
xi. SAP Supplier Lifecycle Management (SRM)
xii. Environmental Health and Safety Management (EHSM)
xiii. Commercial Project Management

xiv. Industry Solutions (Utilities, Telco, CWM)
xv. Portfolio and Project Management
xvi. Agency Business

Perform pre-checks by running program **R_S4_PRE_TRANSITION_CHECKS** in client 000, which uses stack.xml output, file from the Maintenance Planner. The program must be run on every system (Sandbox, DEV, QA, and PROD) to be migrated to S/4HANA. The overall resulting return code must be 4 or lower otherwise, the Software Update Manager (SUM) cannot migrate the system to S/4HANA.

The pre-check program is available in SAP Note 2182725, you can follow the notes for current details.

3.1.1. Relevant SAP Notes for Pre-Checks

3.1.1.1. Logistics Sales and Distribution

In preparation for conversion, the system will check several objects related to the Sales and Distribution code and data structure, according to SD Data Model simplifications and functionality changes. The notes below are required to implement the programs required during the pre-checks:

i. SAP Note 2224436: Pre-Checks for SD Data Model
ii. SAP Note 2188735: Pre-Checks for SD Pricing
iii. SAP Note 2227824: Pre-Checks for SD Revenue Recognition

iv. SAP Note 2205202: Pre-Checks for SD Foreign Trade

3.1.1.2. Logistics Material Management

Implement the following SAP Notes to enable the system carry pre-checks for MM Data Model simplifications and functionality changes.

i. SAP Note 2206932: Pre-Checks for Material Master Data.
ii. SAP Note 2194618: Pre-Checks for MM Inventory Management.
iii. SAP Note 2196203: Pre-Checks for MM Discrete Industries & Mill Products

3.1.1.3. Environment, Health and Safety (EHS) Management Component Prerequisite checks

In S/4HANA, significant simplifications have been made in the Environment, Health and Safety (EHS) component. EHS is not a common module so I am not explaining EHS conversion in detail.

If EHS is currently implemented, implement the following SAP Notes to enable the system to carry pre-checks for EHS Management simplifications changes.

i. SAP Note 2217208: Pre-Checks for EHSM Master Checks
ii. SAP Note 2198401: Pre-Checks for EHS Industrial Hygiene and Safety (EHS-IHS)

3.1.1.4. Product Life-Cycle Management (PLM)

In S/4HANA, significant changes are being made in Product Lifecycle Management. PLM is not a common module so I am not explaining PLM conversion in detail.

If PLM is currently implemented, implement the following SAP Note to enable the system to carry pre-checks for PLM simplifications changes.

SAP Note 2267842: Pre-Checks for Access Control Management (ACM)

3.1.2. Perform Data Consistency Checks

Before conversion, carry out the following technical consistency checks to validate consistency of the data before conversion.

3.1.2.1. FI data consistency checks across indexes and documents

You can perform comparative checks using program **RFINDEX_NACC**. It identifies inconsistencies in financial data across different tables, which must be corrected. If required, contact SAP with error detail for the resolution and I would suggest not to continue with the conversion.

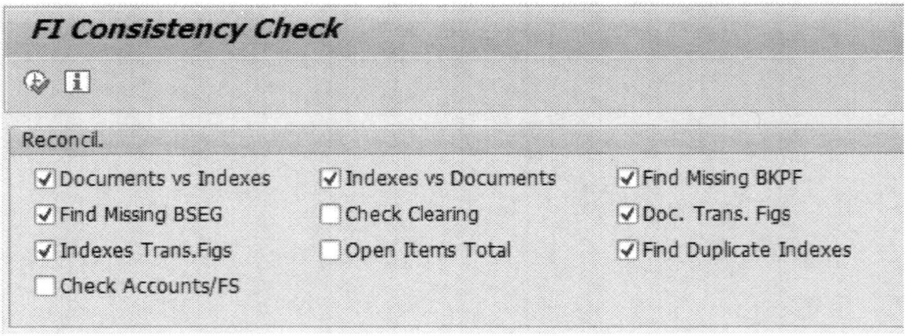
FI Consistency Check
Reconcil.
Documents vs Indexes
Indexes vs Documents
Find Missing BKPF
Find Missing BSEG
Check Clearing
Doc. Trans. Figs
Indexes Trans.Figs
Open Items Total
Find Duplicate Indexes
Check Accounts/FS

If there are differences, the system displays the affected tables and the fields.

3.1.2.2. Reconciliation of General Ledger against Accounts Payable/Receivable

For New General Ledger (G/L) installations, use program **TFC_COMPARE_VZ** to ensure that summary of the G/L matches the totals for Accounts Payable (AP) and Accounts Receivable (AR) sub-ledgers. Execute this report for the last fiscal year/period, using the single document comparison option.

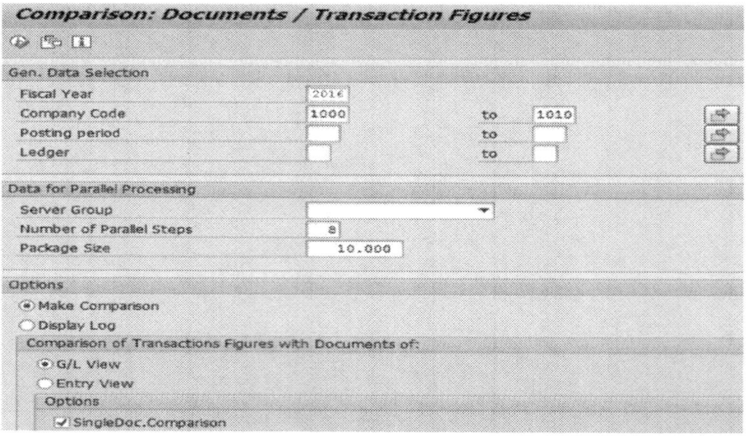
Comparison: Documents / Transaction Figures
Gen. Data Selection
Fiscal Year
2016
Company Code
1000
to
1010
Posting period
to
Ledger
to
Data for Parallel Processing
Server Group
Number of Parallel Steps
8
Package Size
10.000
Options
Make Comparison
Display Log
Comparison of Transactions Figures with Documents of:
G/L View
Entry View
Options
SingleDoc.Comparison

If the source system uses the Classic G/L, use program SAPF190 to reconcile with A/P and A/R subledgers.

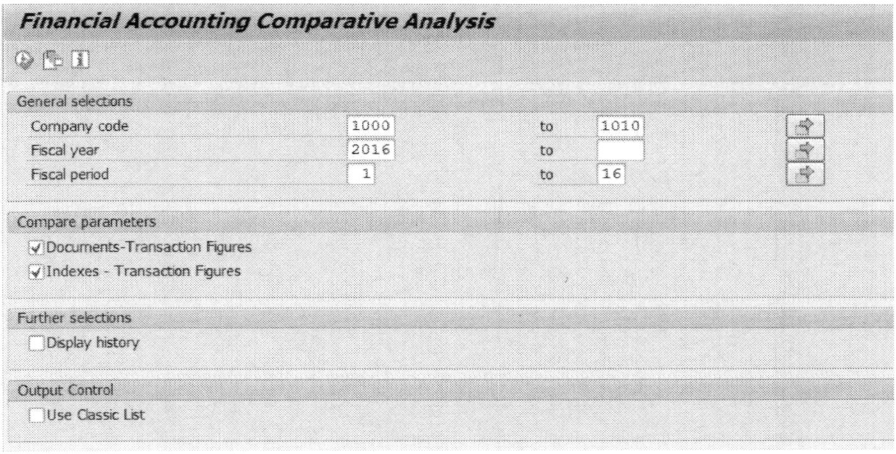
Financial Accounting Comparative Analysis
General selections
Company code
1000
to
1010
Fiscal year
2016
to
Fiscal period
1
to
16
Compare parameters
Documents-Transaction Figures
Indexes - Transaction Figures
Further selections
Display history
Output Control
Use Classic List

3.1.2.3. Reconciliation of General Ledger with Asset Accounting

The classic Asset Accounting sub module (FI-AA) has its own period closing procedures, therefore execute program **RAABST02** to ensure that the last period closed in FI-AA matches with the last period in the General Ledger (FI-GL).

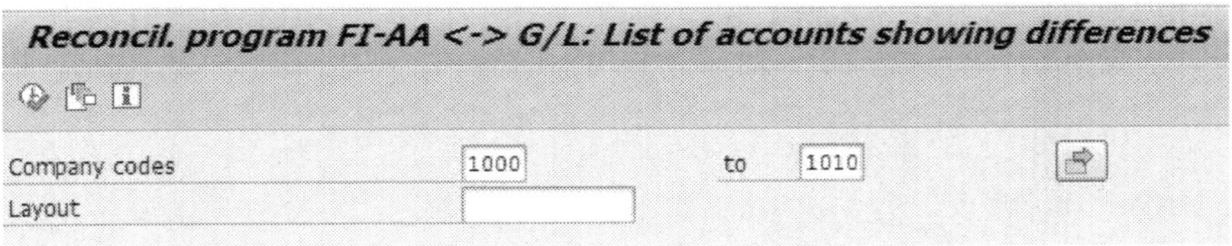
Reconcil. program FI-AA <-> G/L: List of accounts showing differences
Company codes
1000
to
1010
Layout

If the system highlights inconsistencies between asset accounting and general ledger close periods, correct them before conversion. For example, to correct the inconsistency below, perform the Asset Accounting periodic processing and year change for company codes 1000 and 1010 as follows:

i. AJRW - Fiscal Year Change
ii. AFAB – Execute Depreciation
iii. AJAB – Execute Year Closing
iv. ASKB - APC Values Posting

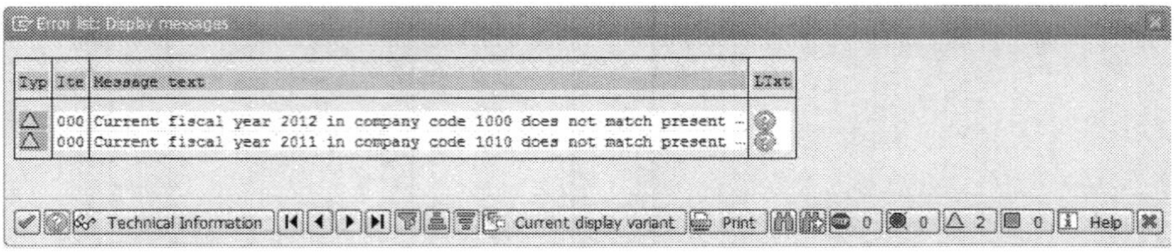
Error list: Display messages
Typ
Ite
Message text
LTxt
000
Current fiscal year 2012 in company code 1000 does not match present
000
Current fiscal year 2011 in company code 1010 does not match present
Technical Information
Current display variant
Print
0
0
2
0
Help

After corrections are done, re-run the consistency report to confirm that no more errors are found.

3.1.2.4. Reconciliation of Ledgers

If converting from new General Ledger, use transaction GCAC (program RGUCOMP4) to compare the ledgers and check that they reconcile. The report must be executed for each fiscal year.

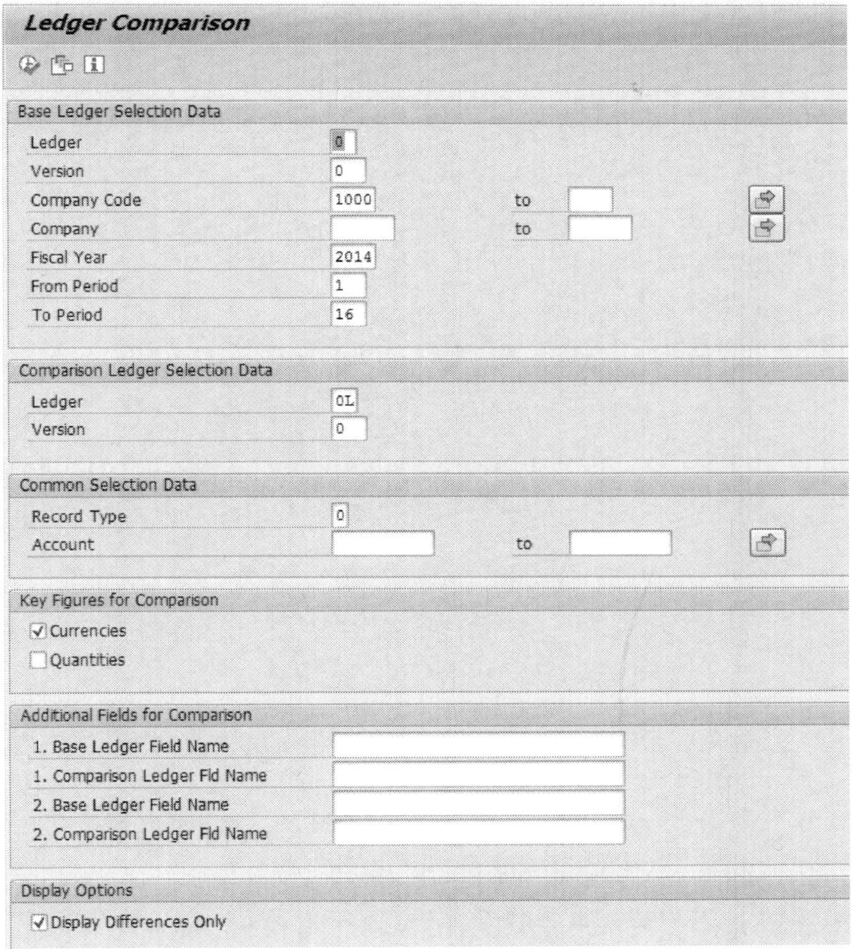
Ledger Comparison
Base Ledger Selection Data
Ledger
0
Version
0
Company Code
1000
to
Company
to
Fiscal Year
2014
From Period
1
To Period
16
Comparison Ledger Selection Data
Ledger
0L
Version
0
Common Selection Data
Record Type
0
Account
to
Key Figures for Comparison
Currencies
Quantities
Additional Fields for Comparison
1. Base Ledger Field Name
1. Comparison Ledger Fld Name
2. Base Ledger Field Name
2. Comparison Ledger Fld Name
Display Options
Display Differences Only

3.1.2.5. Reconciliation of General Ledger with Materials Management

Execute program **RM07MMFI** to validate the summary totals in the general ledger match the totals in the materials management sub-ledger. Run the program for all productive company codes and for current and prior fiscal years.

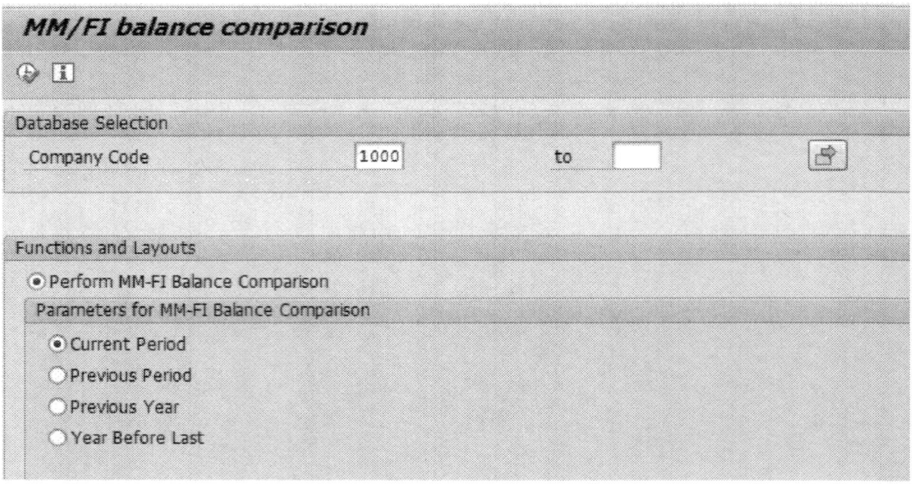
MM/FI balance comparison
Database Selection
Company Code
1000
to
Functions and Layouts
Perform MM-FI Balance Comparison
Parameters for MM-FI Balance Comparison
Current Period
Previous Period
Previous Year
Year Before Last

If there are any inconsistencies found, correct them before moving to the next conversion step.

Inconsistencies between "Value of Materials" and "Value of G/L account" accounts may also be caused by material documents that did not update the totals table, leaving differences between the totals and line items reports FAGLB03 and FAGLL03 for the inventory accounts. Ensure these are corrected before proceeding with conversion.

3.1.3. Period-End Closing Activities

Scheduled conversions should occur only at the end of the period or year. In addition, it is imperative to lock all users in the system who have no period-end close or conversion tasks assigned. Perform the following activities and document the results using the mentioned transaction codes:

i. Lock the Materials Management period - MMPV (program RMMMPERI)

ii. If Classic Asset Accounting, perform asset periodic posting – ASKBN (program RAPERB2000)

iii. Run the Asset Account Depreciation – AFAB (program RAPOST2000)

iv. Completely post or delete outstanding Held Documents – FB50

v. Ensure Balance Carry Forward has been performed for the current year for all ledgers and subledgers:

- FAGLGVTR for the new General Ledger
- F.16 for the classic General Ledger
- AJRW for Asset Accounting
- F.07 for Accounts Receivable and Accounts Payable

vi. Close all prior Fiscal Years, only the current year should be open for all companies – AJAB (program RAJABS00)

vii. Reset valuation marked on open line items by running F.05 (Program SAPF100); maintain a valuation method that resets the valuation in transaction code OB59

viii. Execute all background jobs
ix. Lock all Financial periods – OB52
x. Lock all periods in Controlling – OKP1
xi. Execute the validation program RASFIN_MIGR_PRECHECK and resolve reported issue

3.1.4. Pre-Conversion Business review of Balance and Transactions

Finance users should carry out the reports listed below before the conversion. These reports need to be repeated again after the conversion; to be used as business data validation for the Go/No-go decision point:

i. **General Ledger report**

- Financial Statement - S_ALR_87012284
- General Ledger Balance list - F.08
- General Ledger line items list - FBL3N
- General Ledger line items list (program RFSOPO00 or extract RFBPET00)
- The Compact Document Journal - S_ALR_87012289
- Recurring entry original documents - F.15

ii. **Asset Accounting**

- Asset History Sheet - S_ALR_87011990
- Depreciation reports - AR03 (program RAHAFA_ALV01)

iii. **Controlling**

- Order: Actual/Plan/Variance - S_ALR_87012993
- Cost Center Totals report - S_ALR_87013611

iv. **Accounts Payable**

- Vendor Balances - S_ALR_87012082
- Vendor Line Items - FBL1N
- Vendor Sales -S_ALR_87012093

v. **Accounts Receivable**

- Customer Balances - S_ALR_87012172
- Customer Open Line Items - FBL5N
- Customer Sales - S_ALR_87012186

The reports must provide adequate assurance of the process and enable finance users to sign off the conversion prior to go/no-go decision.

3.1.5. Prepare Business Process Changes for replaced Material Management Transactions

Update business processes using MB* transaction codes to start using transaction MIGO. The following transactions for entering and displaying goods movements (material documents) - called "MB transactions" below - have been replaced by the single-screen transaction MIGO: MB01, MB02, MB03, MB04, MB05, MB0A, MB11, MB1A, MB1B, MB1C, MB31, MBNL, MBRL, MBSF, MBSL, MBST, and MBSU.

3.2. Technical Pre-Conversion

3.2.1. Technical Details of the Conversion

Take into account possible performance decrease during conversion and adjust system parameters if necessary. The increased resource usage comes from the “system switch conversion procedure” in use during conversion.

This procedure installs an instance of the target release (shadow system) in parallel with the current source release system in the same database. The parallel system contains all the software of the target release and is used to perform actions on the target release while the source release is still in productive operation.

3.2.2. Modification Adjustment Planning

Execute transaction SPDD and SPAU to highlight suggested updates to SAP objects to be impacted by S/4HANA conversion. Accept or adjust all modifications to standard SAP objects made available by the system. For QA and Production, do not adjust modifications and enhancements manually; instead, transfer the transport requests exported from the Development

The ADJUSTPRP phase in the Configuration roadmap step prepares the requests from the development system to be transferred. The Software Update Manager reads the umodauto.lst file and prompts for a transport request for capturing the changes.

4. System Conversion

4.1. Preparation for Finance Data Conversion

Perform the following activities to prepare for conversion of Master and Transactional data to the S/4HANA system.

4.1.1. Define message types for posting before and during migration

Define system message to prevent users from posting during conversion to prevent system inconsistencies. Maintain message 150 of work area FINS_FI_MIG to "E" (Error). After completing all conversion steps, changing conversion status to complete will enable users to post in the system.

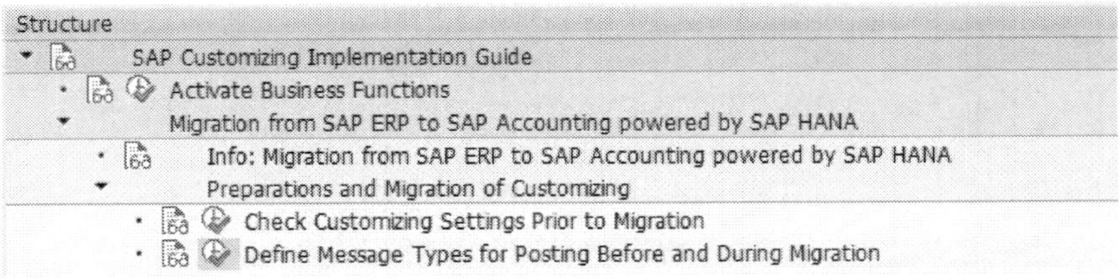
Structure
SAP Customizing Implementation Guide
Activate Business Functions
Migration from SAP ERP to SAP Accounting powered by SAP HANA
Info: Migration from SAP ERP to SAP Accounting powered by SAP HANA
Preparations and Migration of Customizing
Check Customizing Settings Prior to Migration
Define Message Types for Posting Before and During Migration

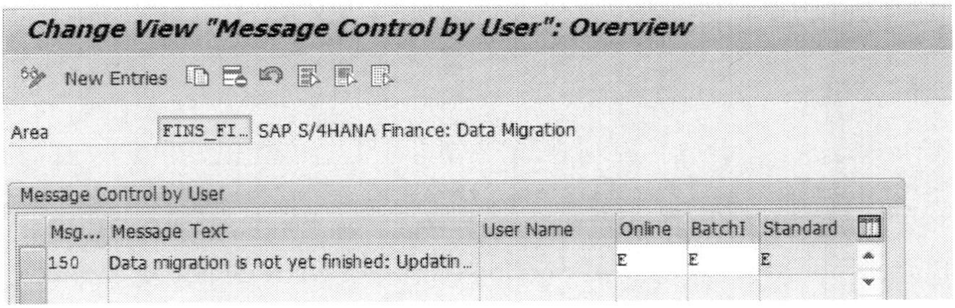
Change View "Message Control by User": Overview
New Entries
Area
FINS_FI...
SAP S/4HANA Finance: Data Migration
Message Control by User
Msg...
Message Text
User Name
Online
BatchI
Standard
150
Data migration is not yet finished: Updatin...
E
E
E

4.1.2. Customizing in General Ledger

Perform the following additional customizations before General Ledger data conversion. If the IMG menu below is not visible as depicted below, activate it by executing the program **RFAGL_SWAP_IMG_NEW**.

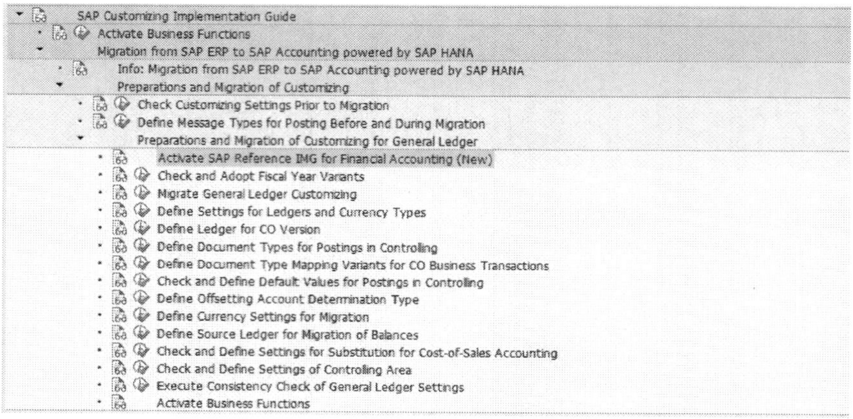
SAP Customizing Implementation Guide
Activate Business Functions
Migration from SAP ERP to SAP Accounting powered by SAP HANA
Info: Migration from SAP ERP to SAP Accounting powered by SAP HANA
Preparations and Migration of Customizing
Check Customizing Settings Prior to Migration
Define Message Types for Posting Before and During Migration
Preparations and Migration of Customizing for General Ledger
Activate SAP Reference IMG for Financial Accounting (New)
Check and Adopt Fiscal Year Variants
Migrate General Ledger Customizing
Define Settings for Ledgers and Currency Types
Define Ledger for CO Version
Define Document Types for Postings in Controlling
Define Document Type Mapping Variants for CO Business Transactions
Check and Define Default Values for Postings in Controlling
Define Offsetting Account Determination Type
Define Currency Settings for Migration
Define Source Ledger for Migration of Balances
Check and Define Settings for Substitution for Cost-of-Sales Accounting
Check and Define Settings of Controlling Area
Execute Consistency Check of General Ledger Settings
Activate Business Functions

4.1.3. Check and Adopt Fiscal Year Variants

The conversion to the Universal Journal requires the same fiscal year variant to be used in Controlling (CO) and Financial Accounting (FI). Execute this report in IMG (Transaction: **FINS_MIG_FYV**) for all productive controlling areas to determine if settings are congruent between Controlling Areas and their assigned Company Codes. If the system highlights an inconsistency, then it's usually best to modify the setting in the company code(s) and not that of the controlling area.

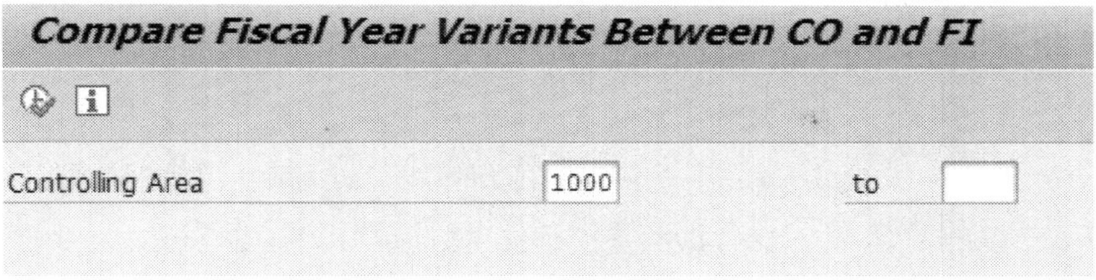
Compare Fiscal Year Variants Between CO and FI
Controlling Area
1000
to

4.1.4. Migrate General Ledger Customizing

Execute this activity (transaction code: **FINS_MIG_LEDGER_CUST**) to migrate existing G/L Ledgers in the source system to the new configuration for S/4HANA Finance. The following settings are migrated:

i. Company code assignments
ii. Currency settings
iii. Fiscal year variant
iv. Open period variant
v. Settings for real-time integration of CO-FI

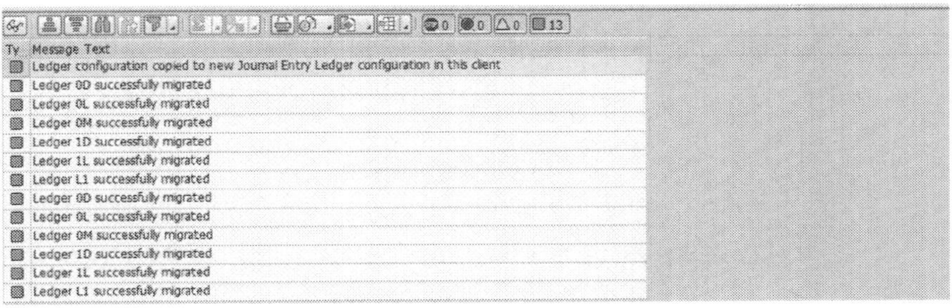
Ty
Message Text
Ledger configuration copied to new Journal Entry Ledger configuration in this client
Ledger 0D successfully migrated
Ledger 0L successfully migrated
Ledger 0M successfully migrated
Ledger 1D successfully migrated
Ledger 1L successfully migrated
Ledger L1 successfully migrated
Ledger 0D successfully migrated
Ledger 0L successfully migrated
Ledger 0M successfully migrated
Ledger 1D successfully migrated
Ledger 1L successfully migrated
Ledger L1 successfully migrated

4.1.5. Define Settings for Ledgers and Currency Types

Perform the following customizing steps in this screen.

i. Define ledgers according to business requirements. Naturally, only one ledger can be defined as leading ledger (standard leading ledger is 0L)

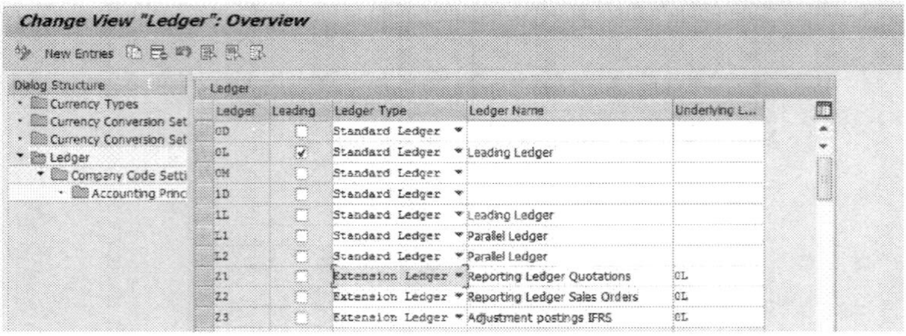
Change View "Ledger": Overview
New Entries
Dialog Structure
Currency Types
Currency Conversion Set
Currency Conversion Set
Ledger
Company Code Setti
Accounting Princ
Ledger
Ledger
Leading
Ledger Type
Ledger Name
Underlying L...
0D
Standard Ledger
0L
Standard Ledger
Leading Ledger
0M
Standard Ledger
1D
Standard Ledger
1L
Standard Ledger
Leading Ledger
L1
Standard Ledger
Parallel Ledger
L2
Standard Ledger
Parallel Ledger
Z1
Extension Ledger
Reporting Ledger Quotations
0L
Z2
Extension Ledger
Reporting Ledger Sales Orders
0L
Z3
Extension Ledger
Adjustment postings IFRS
0L

There are two types of ledgers:

- **Standard**: A standard ledger contains a full set of journal entries for all business transactions.
- **Extension**: An extension ledger is assigned to a standard ledger and inherits all journal entries of the standard ledger for reporting. Postings made explicitly to the extension ledger are visible in that extension ledger but not in the underlying standard ledger. This concept can be used to avoid duplication of journal entries if many business transactions are valid for both ledgers and only a few adjustments are required in the extension ledger.

Note: Since the ledger configuration must be consistent between all company codes that use the same Asset Accounting Chart of Depreciation, it may be necessary to add ledgers to existing company codes. Additional ledgers may also be needed to manage the shifted fiscal year in Asset Accounting (see SAP Note 1951069)

ii. Assign company codes to ledgers and define currency settings and associated fiscal year variants

It is possible to setup 3 additional parallel currencies in addition to the local and group currencies, as shown in the figure below:

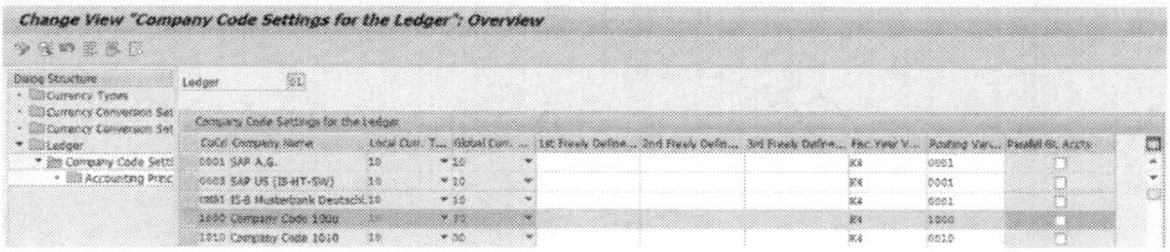
Change View "Company Code Settings for the Ledger": Overview
Ledger
Company Code Settings for the Ledger

iii. Assign accounting principle per unique combination of ledger and company code

If using the parallel accounting by account approach instead of the ledger approach, be sure to check the box "Parallel GL Accounts." It is then possible to assign more than one accounting principle per unique combination of ledger and company code.

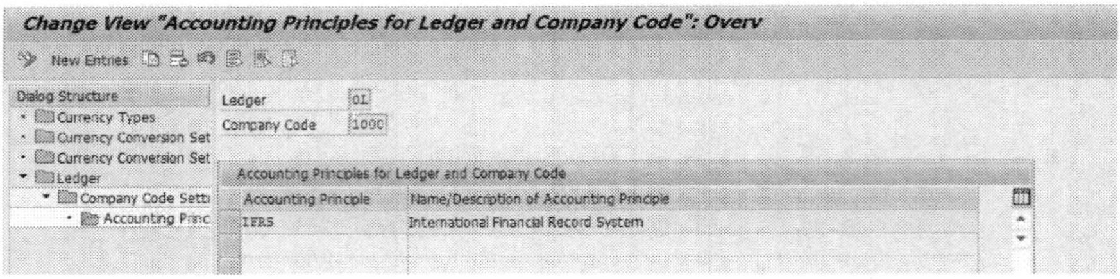
Change View "Accounting Principles for Ledger and Company Code": Overv
New Entries
Dialog Structure
Currency Types
Currency Conversion Set
Currency Conversion Set
Ledger
Company Code Setti
Accounting Princ
Ledger 0L
Company Code 1000
Accounting Principles for Ledger and Company Code
Accounting Principle
Name/Description of Accounting Principle
IFRS
International Financial Record System

4.1.6. Define Ledger for CO Version

Define a ledger that represents Controlling, i.e. a ledger that contains all postings of actual data that is relevant to Controlling. This is done by assigning the version 000 to a ledger at the company code level with the same ledger being used for all company codes.

The current restriction is that the version 000 must be assigned to the leading ledger for all company codes that are assigned to a Controlling area.

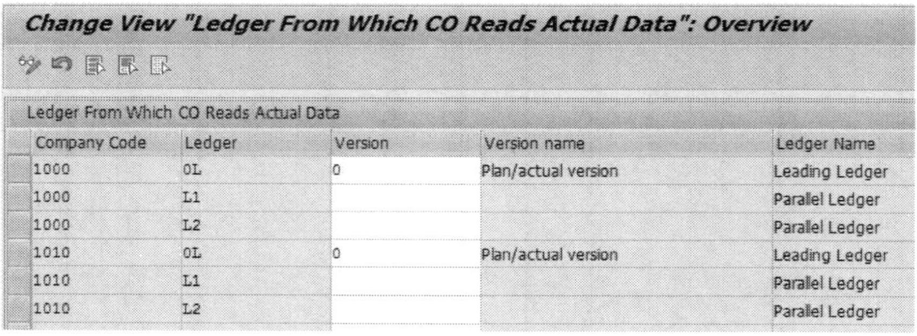
Change View "Ledger From Which CO Reads Actual Data": Overview
Ledger From Which CO Reads Actual Data
Company Code
Ledger
Version
Version name
Ledger Name
1000
0L
0
Plan/actual version
Leading Ledger
1000
L1
Parallel Ledger
1000
L2
Parallel Ledger
1010
0L
0
Plan/actual version
Leading Ledger
1010
L1
Parallel Ledger
1010
L2
Parallel Ledger

4.1.7. Define Document Type Mapping Variants for CO Business Transactions

Define a mapping variant that maps CO business transactions to document types. This mapping must be done for all CO business transactions that do actual postings.

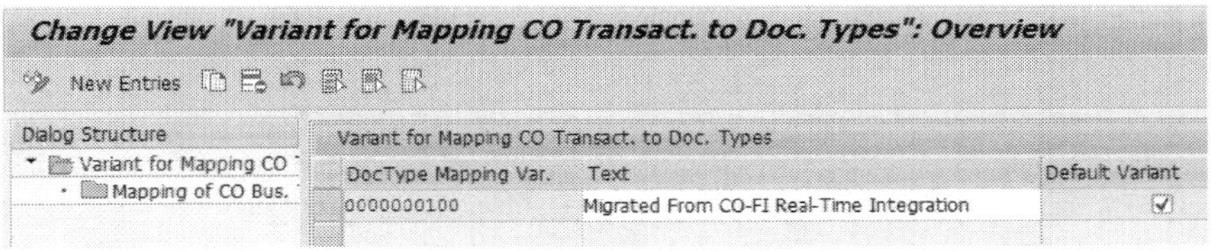
Change View "Variant for Mapping CO Transact. to Doc. Types": Overview
New Entries
Dialog Structure
Variant for Mapping CO
Mapping of CO Bus.
Variant for Mapping CO Transact. to Doc. Types
DocType Mapping Var.
Text
Default Variant
0000000100
Migrated From CO-FI Real-Time Integration

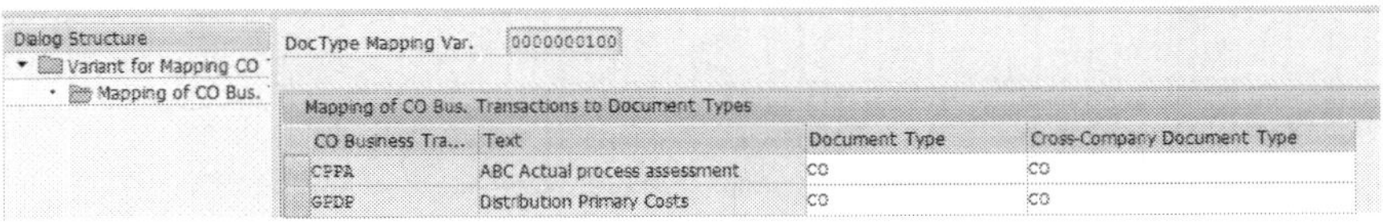
Dialog Structure
Variant for Mapping CO
Mapping of CO Bus.
DocType Mapping Var.
0000000100
Mapping of CO Bus. Transactions to Document Types
CO Business Tra...
Text
Document Type
Cross-Company Document Type
CPPA
ABC Actual process assessment
CO
CO
GEDP
Distribution Primary Costs
CO
CO

4.1.8. Check and Define Default Values for Postings in Controlling

Define document type mapping variant and default ledger group for use in CO business transactions whose user interfaces do not provide an input screen. If a default ledger group is not defined, all CO postings will be done to all ledgers in the GL.

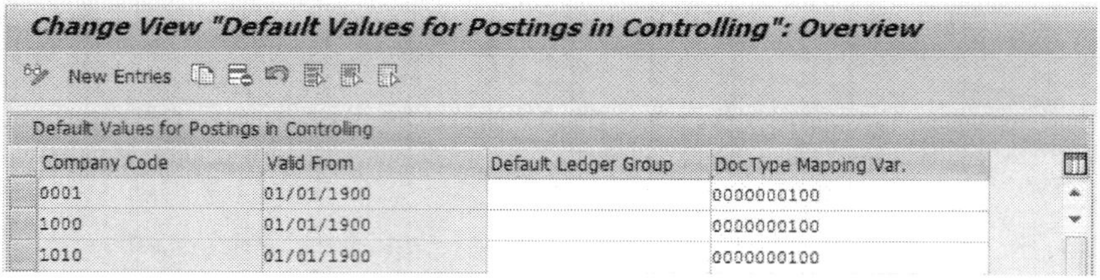
Change View "Default Values for Postings in Controlling": Overview
New Entries
Default Values for Postings in Controlling
Company Code
Valid From
Default Ledger Group
DocType Mapping Var.
0001
01/01/1900
0000000100
1000
01/01/1900
0000000100
1010
01/01/1900
0000000100

4.1.9. Define Offsetting Account Determination Type

Define how the system calculates the offsetting account in all applications. SAP recommends choosing the option "As case 2, but including line items generated automatically."

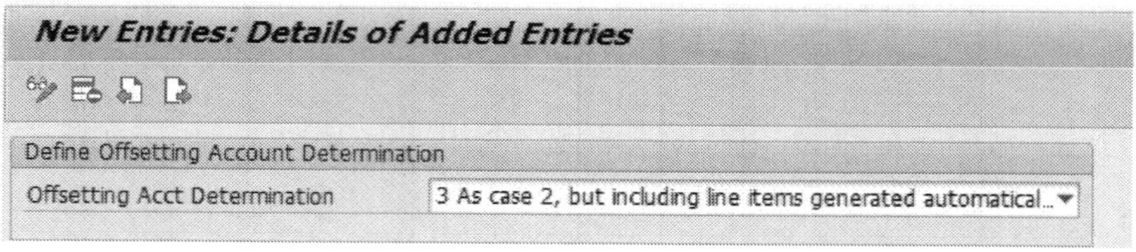
New Entries: Details of Added Entries
Define Offsetting Account Determination
Offsetting Acct Determination
3 As case 2, but including line items generated automatical...

4.1.10. Define Currency Settings for Migration

Maintain exchange rate types for utilization in currency translations by the conversion process when currency amounts are available in other currencies only. The system uses the exchange rate types to fill the amount in the company code currency for all items of the universal journal. If the exchange rate type is not maintained, affected items are migrated with amount zero.

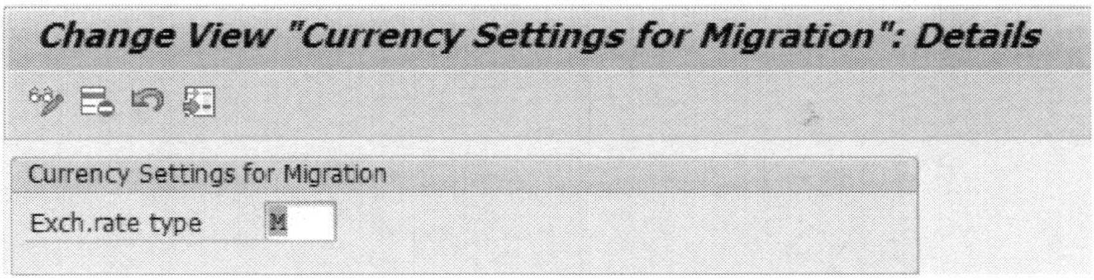
Change View "Currency Settings for Migration": Details
Currency Settings for Migration
Exch.rate type
M

4.1.11. Define Source Ledger for Migration of Balance

Define the source ledger (and by doing so the source database table) of the balances for General Ledger Accounting. In this activity, the source and target ledgers do not need to have the same name to make the necessary assignments.

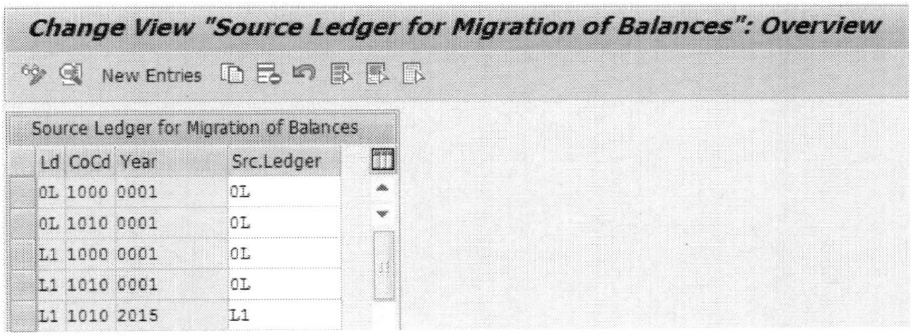
Change View "Source Ledger for Migration of Balances": Overview
New Entries
Source Ledger for Migration of Balances
Ld CoCd Year Src.Ledger
0L 1000 0001 0L
0L 1010 0001 0L
L1 1000 0001 0L
L1 1010 0001 0L
L1 1010 2015 L1

4.1.12. Execute Consistency Check of General Ledger Settings

Execute transaction FINS_CUST_CONS_CHK (program FINS_CUST_CONSISTENCY_CHECK) report to validate consistency of the ledger settings.

Note: This check must run without error messages, as illustrated in the figure below, before conversion of transaction data. If the check raises issues with the template company codes, which are not productive, these can be excluded by setting the flag "Template" in table V_001_TEMPLATE.

Ty. Message Text
Currency conversion settings for ledger / company assigment checked in this client
Check passed

4.2. Running Software Update Manager (SUM)

The Software Update Manager (SUM) tool converts the system to SAP S/4HANA 1610 and the steps below should be followed. As of S/4HANA 1610 the latest SUM 1.0 SP20 was used for conversion.

4.2.1. Prepare directory for unpacking SUM

Prepare the standard path /usr/sap/<SID> for unpacking SUM and ensure there's a minimum of 500MB (depending on the packages included) free space available.

4.2.2. Download and Unpack SUM

Download the latest version of SUM from the main Software Logistics Toolset page from: http://service.sap.com/sltoolset

Unpack the SUM package with the following command under

<sid>adm user: SAPCAR –xvf <download directory>/<path>/<Archive>.SAR -R /usr/sap/<sid>

4.2.3. Register SUM in SAP Host Agent

Register SUM in SAP Host Agent so that the operations and commands to the updated system are executed using SAP Host Agent mechanisms.

i. To start SUM, enter the following with 'root' user:

cd /usr/sap/<SID>/SUM./STARTUP confighostagent <SID>

ii. Upgrade Host Agent to the latest version if needed:

./saphostexec -upgrade -archive /tmp/SAPHOSTAGENTxx_xx-xxxxxxx.SAR

iii. In the web browser, enter the following URL:

https://<hostname>:1129/lmsl/sumabap/<SID>/doc/sluigui

or

http://<hostname>:1128/lmsl/sumabap/<SID>/doc/sluigui

4.2.4. Execute the Extraction Roadmap Step

1
Extraction
2
3
4
5
6

iv. Include stack.xml file that was generated by the SAP Maintenance Planner

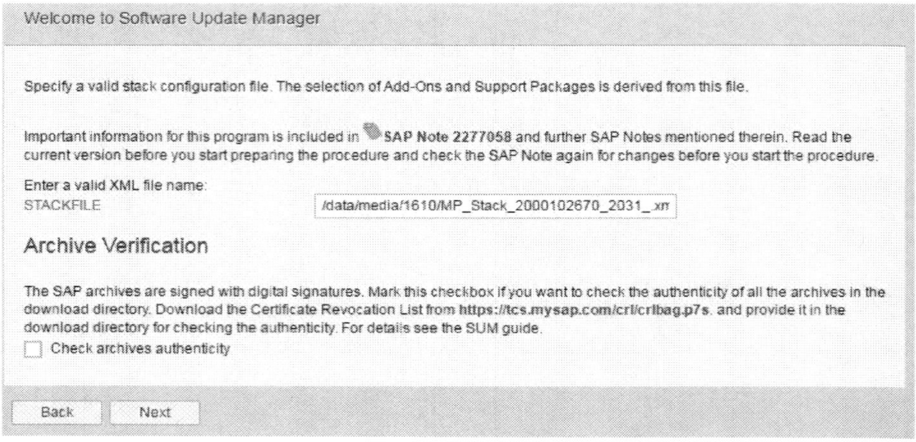
Welcome to Software Update Manager
Specify a valid stack configuration file. The selection of Add-Ons and Support Packages is derived from this file.
Important information for this program is included in SAP Note 2277058 and further SAP Notes mentioned therein. Read the current version before you start preparing the procedure and check the SAP Note again for changes before you start the procedure.
Enter a valid XML file name:
STACKFILE
/data/media/1610/MP_Stack_2000102670_2031_.xr
Archive Verification
The SAP archives are signed with digital signatures. Mark this checkbox if you want to check the authenticity of all the archives in the download directory. Download the Certificate Revocation List from https://tcs.mysap.com/crl/crlbag.p7s. and provide it in the download directory for checking the authenticity. For details see the SUM guide.
Check archives authenticity
Back
Next

v. Mount Directories for the Data Carriers (Phase KEY_CHK)

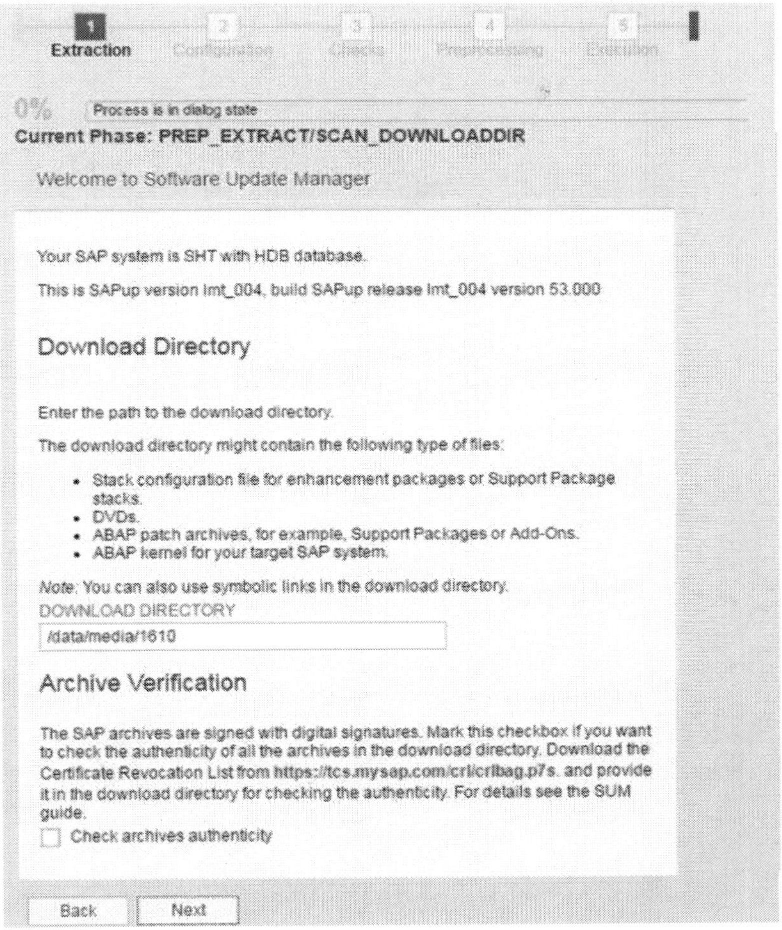
1
Extraction
2
3
4
5
0%
Process is in dialog state
Current Phase: PREP_EXTRACT/SCAN_DOWNLOADDIR
Welcome to Software Update Manager
Your SAP system is SHT with HDB database.
This is SAPup version lmt_004, build SAPup release lmt_004 version 53.000
Download Directory
Enter the path to the download directory.
The download directory might contain the following type of files:
Stack configuration file for enhancement packages or Support Package stacks.
DVDs.
ABAP patch archives, for example, Support Packages or Add-Ons.
ABAP kernel for your target SAP system.
Note: You can also use symbolic links in the download directory.
DOWNLOAD DIRECTORY
/data/media/1610
Archive Verification
The SAP archives are signed with digital signatures. Mark this checkbox if you want to check the authenticity of all the archives in the download directory. Download the Certificate Revocation List from https://tcs.mysap.com/crl/crlbag.p7s. and provide it in the download directory for checking the authenticity. For details see the SUM guide.
Check archives authenticity
Back
Next

vi. If the following error regarding HANA client is obtained, patch HANA client to a newer version.

(!) List of tools failing the checks

SUM-Phase: PREP_INPUT/TOOLCHECKXML_DBCLI

ERROR:
Symptom:
The upgrade procedure needs a patched version of the tool listed below.
Each tool in question was called without explicit path, this is determined by the OS from the environment variable "PATH".

Necessary Action

For the Current Path:
Download the latest unicode executable available from the SAP Service Marketplace and update it in the current path before you continue.

List of failing tools:

Kernel Type:	cur	Current tool path			
-	Code Page:	Unicode			
-	Action:	Update the current path			
-	Tool:	hanaclient	Solvable issue		
-		Tool Path	/usr/sap/SHT/hdbclient/hdbsql		
-		Variable	Current	Required	E
-		*Release*	1.00	1.00	-
-		*Version*	102	**120**	*
-		*Patchlevel*	03	**42**	*

1. Download HANA Client
2. Backup old hdbclient directory
3. Unpack HANA Client SAR file
4. Install new HANA DB client using 'hdbinst –a client' command

4.2.5. Execute the Configuration Step in Roadmap

i. Select Pre-configuration mode

Plan the conversion to fit specific requirements regarding the availability of the SAP system. Choose the most appropriate pre-configuration mode to fit these requirements.

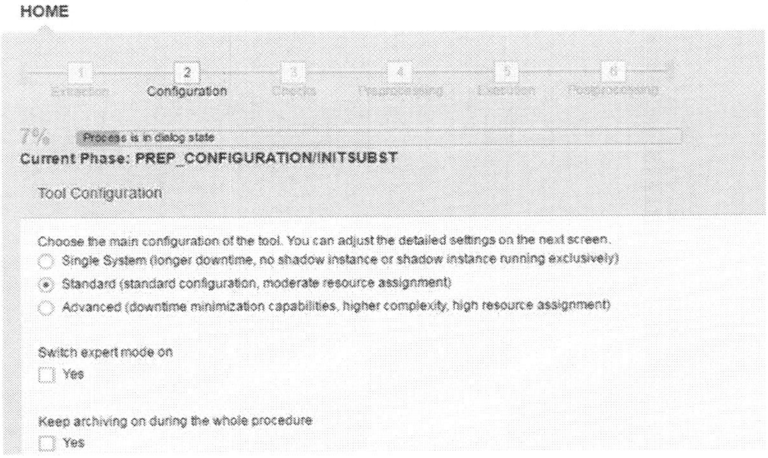
HOME
2
Configuration
7%
Process is in dialog state
Current Phase: PREP_CONFIGURATION/INITSUBST
Tool Configuration
Choose the main configuration of the tool. You can adjust the detailed settings on the next screen.
Single System (longer downtime, no shadow instance or shadow instance running exclusively)
Standard (standard configuration, moderate resource assignment)
Advanced (downtime minimization capabilities, higher complexity, high resource assignment)
Switch expert mode on
Yes
Keep archiving on during the whole procedure
Yes

i. Enter the password of DDIC user (Phase PROFREAD)

Enter the password for DDIC user in Client 000. This password is needed for the RFC connection to the SAP system. To be able to perform all necessary actions, DDIC needs the authorization SAP_ALL.

ii. Enter the password for SAP HANA database user SYSTEM (Phase DBQUERY_PRE)

SUM needs the password for the SAP HANA database user SYSTEM.

iii. Verify and Update of Tool Versions (Phase TOOLVERSION_INI)

SUM checks the tool versions in the system (SAP kernel patch level, the TP version, and the date of R3TRANS). If necessary, SUM prompts to switch the SAP kernel or the other tools to a version and patch level released for the conversion.

iv. Add-on Check

Uninstall or delete any add-on that is not supported for S/4HANA 1610 using transaction SAINT. If uninstalling is not possible, create a SAP customer message using component XX-SER-REL - SAP notes 2214409.

Note: Unsupported add-ons will cause issues during upgrade

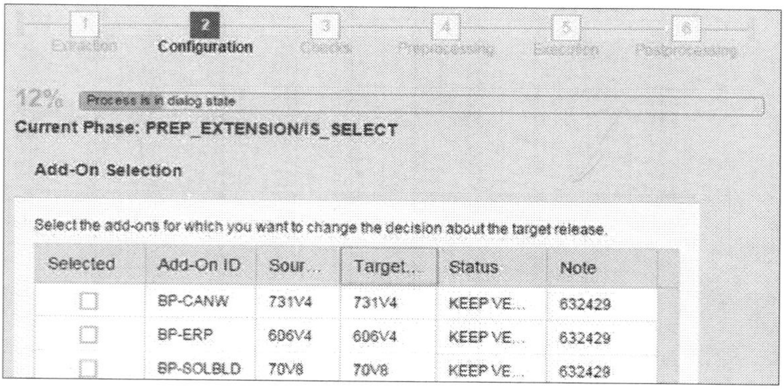
Configuration
12%
Process is in dialog state
Current Phase: PREP_EXTENSION/IS_SELECT
Add-On Selection
Select the add-ons for which you want to change the decision about the target release.
Selected
Add-On ID
Sour...
Target...
Status
Note
BP-CANW
731V4
731V4
KEEP VE...
632429
BP-ERP
606V4
606V4
KEEP VE...
632429
BP-SOLBLD
70V8
70V8
KEEP VE...
632429

```
3 ETN245 The following import prerequisites of OCS package "SAPK-664AGINBPERP" are not met:
3 ETN264   In (alternative) prerequisite set "01":
3WETN491 Prerequisite software component "SAP_APPL" Release "606" is not installed
2EETN085X"The following component versions" "were decided to remain unchanged" "during the update/upgrade process." " "
```

4.2.6. Execute the Checks Roadmap Step

i. Start the Application-Specific Conversion Toolbox

Start the Application-Specific Update toolbox (ASU toolbox) using transaction /ASU/CONVERSION. The system loads the XML file (ASU.XML) contained in the SUM directory, generates a task list, and branches to the task list maintenance. For more information, see SAP Note 1000009.

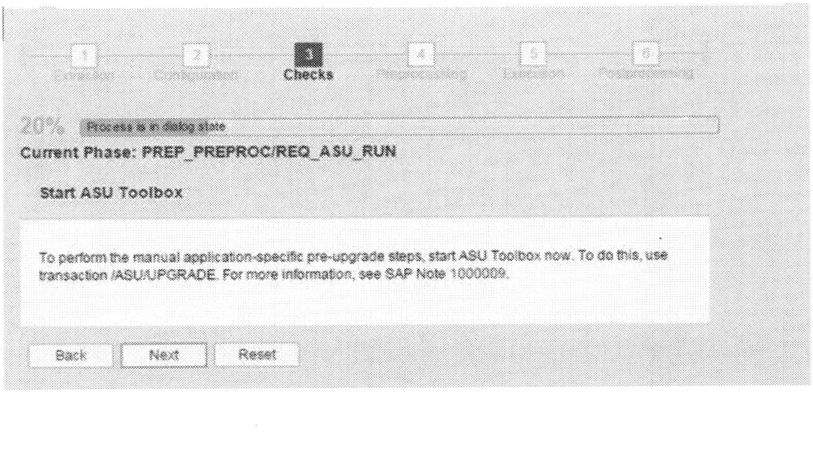
Checks
20%
Process is in dialog state
Current Phase: PREP_PREPROC/REQ_ASU_RUN
Start ASU Toolbox
To perform the manual application-specific pre-upgrade steps, start ASU Toolbox now. To do this, use transaction /ASU/UPGRADE. For more information, see SAP Note 1000009.
Back
Next
Reset

ii. At the end of the Checks roadmap step, SUM displays the results of the system check. The entries can be error messages, information, or prompts for user actions.

4.2.7. Execute the Pre-processing Road Map Step

i. SPAU Fill Level Display (Phase PREP_PARSETUP/SPAU_FILL_LEVEL_DEC)

In this phase, SUM checks for SAP Notes and repository objects that were modified but not adjusted in the transactions SPDD and SPAU in previous updates. If such objects are detected, the phase SPAU_FILL_LEVEL_DEC displays the dialog open actions in transaction SPDD and SPAU. This dialog offers the possibility to complete all outstanding modification adjustments at an early stage of the conversion to reduce the adjustment effort needed later on.
If performing the current update on the Development system, SAP strongly recommends performing the following actions:

1. Confirm all obsolete Notes
2. Reset all non-adjusted objects with active SAP version to SAP standard versions
3. Carry out the outstanding modification adjustments

Afterwards, release the resulting workbench request into the system landscape before continuing with the current update procedure.

In the Development system, use the program **RSUPG_AUTO_ADJ_SPAU** to retrieve the non-adjusted objects that can be reset to the SAP original version. It writes a detailed list to a log file.

If using the automatic reset, note the following:

1. Import the workbench request, which is required for this automatic adjustment, into the subsequent systems before starting the update of these systems.
2. Do not include this workbench request as single change request or as SPDD/SPAU transport request during the update.

ii. ABAP Workbench Locking (Phase LOCKEU_PRE)

If using pre-configuration mode standard or advanced, SUM asks whether the ABAP Workbench is to be locked on all SAP instances now or in phase REPACHK2.

This lock is needed to prevent development objects (ABAP reports, table definitions, and so on) from being changed during the conversion, since those modifications would be lost. The SAP system in productive operation can continue to be used after locking ABAP Workbench. However, it is not possible to perform any more transports into or out of the SAP system.

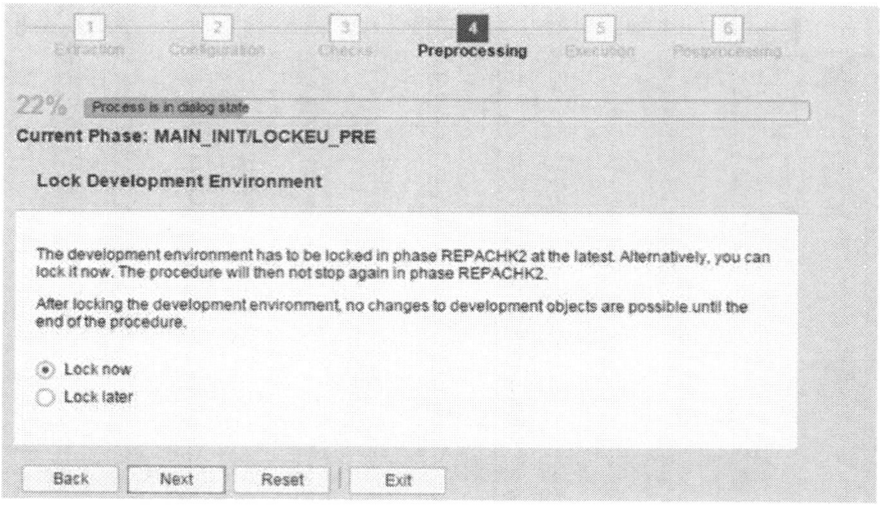
Preprocessing
22%
Process is in dialog state
Current Phase: MAIN_INIT/LOCKEU_PRE
Lock Development Environment
The development environment has to be locked in phase REPACHK2 at the latest. Alternatively, you can lock it now. The procedure will then not stop again in phase REPACHK2.
After locking the development environment, no changes to development objects are possible until the end of the procedure.
Lock now
Lock later
Back
Next
Reset
Exit

iii. Unreleased Repairs and Corrections (Phase REPACHK2)

This phase displays all the repairs and corrections that are not released and writes them to the REPACHK2.LOG file. Before proceeding, release and confirm all the open repairs; otherwise, the objects in them are locked.

iv. Modification Adjustment and Activation (ACT_UPG)

Depending on the results of the ADJUSTCHK phase, SUM may prompt at the beginning of this phase to adjust modifications to ABAP Dictionary objects so that they correspond to the new SAP standard version of the objects.

The ACT_UPG phase can be long, particularly when several modifications to the SAP system were made or included a lot of support packages. This is because the program **RADMASDSC** calculates the dependent objects and the activation sequence for all ABAP Dictionary objects that need to be activated.

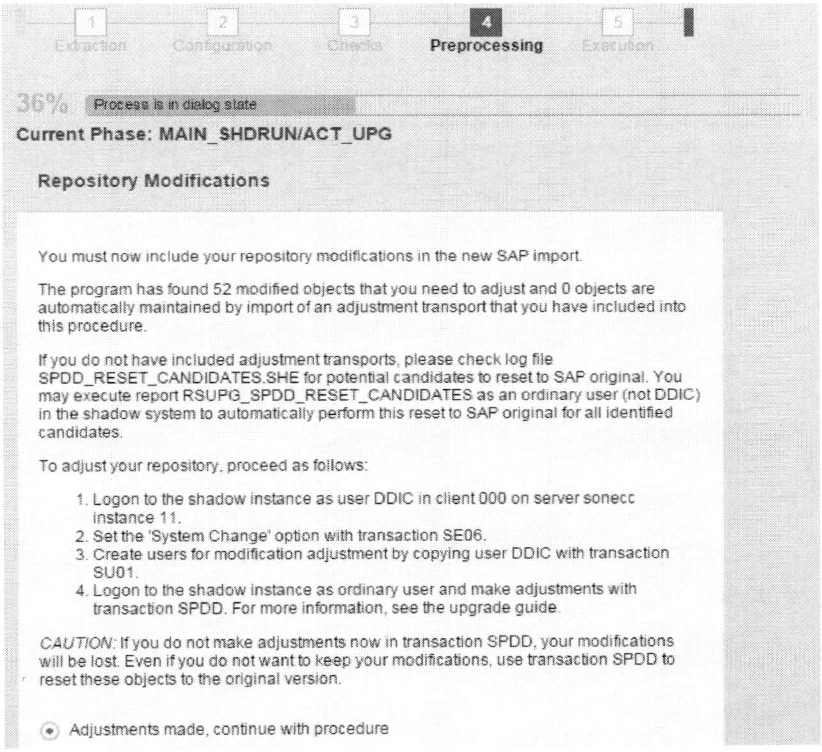
1
Extraction
2
Configuration
3
Checks
4
Preprocessing
5
Execution
36%
Process is in dialog state
Current Phase: MAIN_SHDRUN/ACT_UPG
Repository Modifications
You must now include your repository modifications in the new SAP import.
The program has found 52 modified objects that you need to adjust and 0 objects are automatically maintained by import of an adjustment transport that you have included into this procedure.
If you do not have included adjustment transports, please check log file SPDD_RESET_CANDIDATES.SHE for potential candidates to reset to SAP original. You may execute report RSUPG_SPDD_RESET_CANDIDATES as an ordinary user (not DDIC) in the shadow system to automatically perform this reset to SAP original for all identified candidates.
To adjust your repository, proceed as follows:
1. Logon to the shadow instance as user DDIC in client 000 on server sonecc instance 11.
2. Set the 'System Change' option with transaction SE06.
3. Create users for modification adjustment by copying user DDIC with transaction SU01.
4. Logon to the shadow instance as ordinary user and make adjustments with transaction SPDD. For more information, see the upgrade guide.
CAUTION: If you do not make adjustments now in transaction SPDD, your modifications will be lost. Even if you do not want to keep your modifications, use transaction SPDD to reset these objects to the original version.
Adjustments made, continue with procedure

To make adjustments, proceed as follows:

1. On the SUM GUI, choose option to perform a modification adjustment.

2. Add an entry for the shadow instance to the SAP Logon using SM59.
3. Log on to the shadow instance as user DDIC with the DDIC password of the original system. Only the users DDIC and SAP* exist in the shadow instance.
4. To set the system change option, call transaction SE06. Perform the following actions: Set the global setting, the software components, and the SAP namespace to Modifiable.
5. Call transaction SU01 to create one or more users to perform the modification adjustment.
6. Log on to the shadow instance with one of the new users.
7. Modification adjustment of ABAP Dictionary objects has to be performed in client 000.

Correct all activation errors in modified ABAP Dictionary objects because follow-up activities after the update might rely on the correctness of these objects. All changes to an ABAP Dictionary object during the ACT_UPG phase are automatically recorded in a transport request. For SAP objects modified in transaction SPDD, the SAP system creates the transport request automatically, as mentioned above. For customer-defined objects, however, create a transport request and use it as a single change request in the subsequent system during the update.

v. Preparation of SAP System for Downtime (Phase DOWNCONF*)

At the end of the Preprocessing roadmap step, SUM prompts in phase DOWNCONF_DTTRANS to perform actions that prepare the SAP system for the downtime.

1. Make sure that all production work in the SAP system is stopped and no users are logged on to the SAP system.
2. Make sure that no scheduled batch jobs can start and await regular completion of currently running jobs. SUM automatically executes the report BTCTRNS1 before the update starts. This report transfers all jobs with the status 'Released' to the status 'Suspended'. After the update, reschedule jobs using program **BTCTRNS2**.
3. Isolate the primary application server instance.
4. Choose OK to proceed to the next screen.
5. SUM stops the primary application server instance.
6. Before entering the downtime, perform back up database, directory /usr/sap/<SID> including the update directory, and <sid>adm home directory for restore.
7. Make sure HANA log mode is 'Overwrite' to reduce the log backups during conversion.

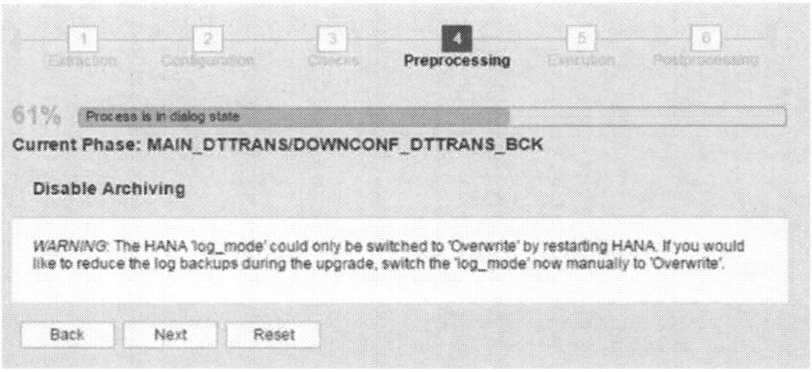
Preprocessing
61%
Process is in dialog state
Current Phase: MAIN_DTTRANS/DOWNCONF_DTTRANS_BCK
Disable Archiving
WARNING: The HANA 'log_mode' could only be switched to 'Overwrite' by restarting HANA. If you would like to reduce the log backups during the upgrade, switch the 'log_mode' now manually to 'Overwrite'.
Back
Next
Reset

4.2.8. Execute the Execution (Downtime) Roadmap Step

i. If issues with "/IWFND/I_MED_SRH" table index is found during Execution roadmap step, refer SAP note 2378526: "/IWFND/I_MED_SRH" table index issue during system upgrade. The index can be deleted during upgrade and recreated after the upgrade is complete.

1. Unlock system using tp command (for details refer SAP note 1901463: How to unlock the SAP system to perform correction(s) during an upgrade)
2. Delete unique index of "/IWFND/I_MED_SRH" table using SE14
3. Lock system using tp command
4. Recreate the deleted index after upgrade is complete

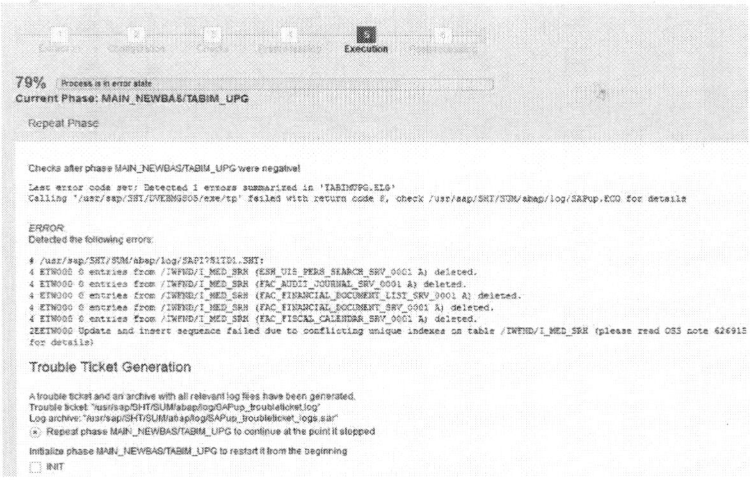
Execution
79% Process is in error state
Current Phase: MAIN_NEWBAS/TABIM_UPG
Repeat Phase
Checks after phase MAIN_NEWBAS/TABIM_UPG were negative!
Last error code set: Detected 1 errors summarized in 'TABIMUPG.ELG'
Calling '/usr/sap/SHT/UVERMG805/exe/tp' failed with return code 8, check /usr/sap/SHT/SUM/abap/log/SAPup.ECO for details
ERROR
Detected the following errors:
/usr/sap/SHT/SUM/abap/log/SAPI?S1TD1.SHT:
4 ETW000 0 entries from /IWFND/I_MED_SRH (ESH_UIS_PERS_SEARCH_SRV_0001 A) deleted.
4 ETW000 0 entries from /IWFND/I_MED_SRH (FAC_AUDIT_JOURNAL_SRV_0001 A) deleted.
4 ETW000 0 entries from /IWFND/I_MED_SRH (FAC_FINANCIAL_DOCUMENT_LIST_SRV_0001 A) deleted.
4 ETW000 0 entries from /IWFND/I_MED_SRH (FAC_FINANCIAL_DOCUMENT_SRV_0001 A) deleted.
4 ETW000 0 entries from /IWFND/I_MED_SRH (FAC_FISCAL_CALENDAR_SRV_0001 A) deleted.
2EETW000 Update and insert sequence failed due to conflicting unique indexes on table /IWFND/I_MED_SRH (please read OSS note 626915 for details)
Trouble Ticket Generation
A trouble ticket and an archive with all relevant log files have been generated.
Trouble ticket: "/usr/sap/SHT/SUM/abap/log/SAPup_troubleticket.log"
Log archive: "/usr/sap/SHT/SUM/abap/log/SAPup_troubleticket_logs.sar"
Repeat phase MAIN_NEWBAS/TABIM_UPG to continue at the point it stopped
Initialize phase MAIN_NEWBAS/TABIM_UPG to restart it from the beginning
INIT

ii. Manual Actions for the ASCS Instance (Phase REQ_ASCS_SWITCH)

If running the ASCS instance on a separate host (for example, in a high availability environment) and the operating system of the host is different from that of the primary application server instance, the system prompts to install the latest SAP kernel on the host with the ASCS instance.

iii. Archiving and Backup (Phase STARTSAP_PUPG)

Make a full backup of the database. If archiving has been deactivated, the system does not change the archiving mode of the database.

4.2.9. Make Entries for the Post-Processing Roadmap Step

i. Modification Adjustment of Repository Objects (Phase SPAUINFO)

If modifications have been made to programs, screens or interfaces (GUIs), adjust them with transaction SPAU. Modification adjustments can be done immediately or after the update is finished. If adjusting the modifications now, SUM exports the related transport request to the transport directory and registers it for transport in the umodauto.lst file. Using this file, SUM can integrate the transport into subsequent updates.

After the update is completed, the system allows 14 days to execute transaction SPAU without the object registration key being checked (SAP Software Change Registration) for the objects modified.

ii. Saving Log Files (Phase SAVELOGS)

SUM saves selected log files and control files. If there are problems after the update, SAP Support can use these files for error analysis. The files are saved in the following directory: /usr/sap/trans/conversion/<SID>/<target release of SAP Basis>

4.3. Post Conversion Technical Activities

4.3.1. Generating Loads

For objects that are new in the SAP system after the update, use transaction SGEN to create the loads. When an ABAP program is called, a load is automatically generated if one does not already exist. This may, however, impair performance in a production system. To avoid this, generate the missing loads using the option "Regenerate" transaction code SGEN after SAP System conversion but before going live.

The additional database space needed to generate ABAP loads is not added automatically to the space requirements reported in the Checks roadmap step. In addition, space approximately the size of table REPOSRC will be needed.

If regenerating invalidated loads after the update, use program **RSGENINVLAS** (until SAP Basis 7.02 SP08) or **RSGENINVLASM** (as of SAP Basis 7.02 SP09). This report regenerates all invalidated ABAP loads only.

SUM has 3 options in Configuration roadmap step to run SGEN. ABAP loads can be generated on shadow system during uptime (Pre-processing roadmap step) or can be generated after conversion.

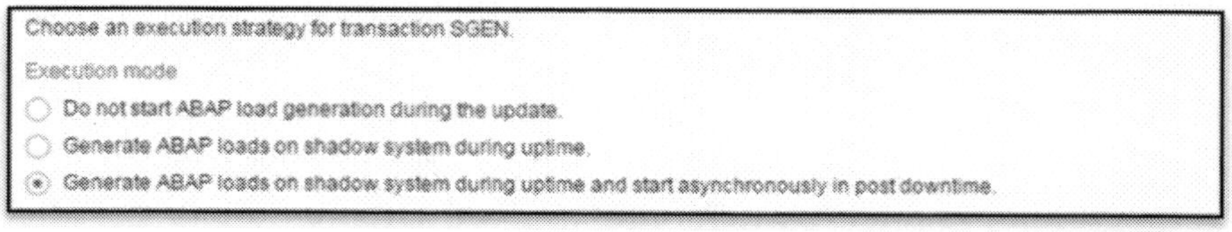
Choose an execution strategy for transaction SGEN.
Execution mode
Do not start ABAP load generation during the update.
Generate ABAP loads on shadow system during uptime.
Generate ABAP loads on shadow system during uptime and start asynchronously in post downtime.

4.3.2. Performing Follow-Up Activities for Application Link Enabling (ALE)

If using Application Link Enabling (ALE) Shared Master Data Management, migrate the change pointers to the new table BDCP2 after the update. Until change pointers are migrated, both the former and the new table are used. For performance reasons, migrate the change pointers as soon as possible after the update.

To check which message types are affected and migrate:

i. Run program RBDCPMIG_ALL_WITHOUT_MIG_FLAG in test mode
ii. Decide whether to run the report for all message types at once or separately
iii. Run program **RBDCPMIG_ALL_WITHOUT_MIG_FLAG** in production mode

4.3.3. Transport Management System: Distributing the Configuration

After an update, distribute the information about the new release to all systems in the transport domain.

i. Log on to the system that is configured as the domain controller
ii. Call transaction STMS and choose Overview -> Systems
iii. Select the system that has been updated and choose SAP System -> Update Configuration
iv. Choose Extras -> Distribute and Activate Configuration

4.3.4. Performing Follow-Up Activities for SAP Solution Manager

In the System Landscape Directory (SLD), check whether the system landscape is up-to-date. To do this, check whether the newest software component versions are assigned to the relevant technical systems in the system landscape. After having verified that the system information in the SLD is up-to-date, the system needs some time (up to 24 hours) to also update the system information in SAP Solution Manager.

4.4. Customizing new Asset Accounting

4.4.1. Set Status for New Asset Accounting to "In Preparation"

Before commencing conversion activities, set the flag for new Asset Accounting to "In preparation" mode. This setting allows configuration activities for new Asset accounting to be set in motion and ensure that New Asset Accounting is not in activated state.

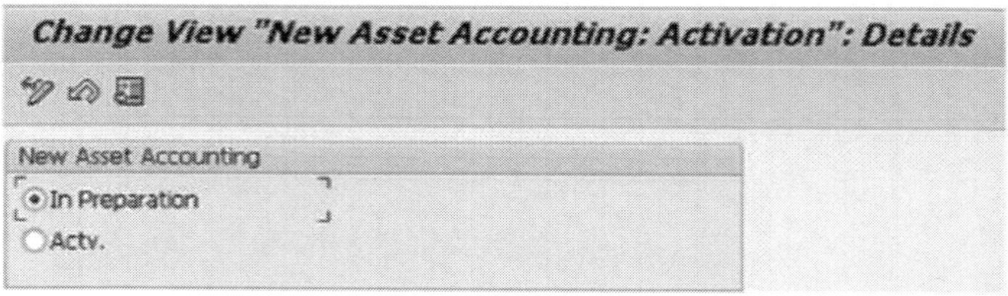
Change View "New Asset Accounting: Activation": Details
New Asset Accounting
In Preparation
Actv.

4.4.2. Change Definitions of Depreciation Areas

Although it is possible to automatically migrate the chart of depreciation using the automated conversion facility provided, manually performing this pre-conversion activity is the recommended approach as it offers flexibility and greater control over the eventual settings. In the automated process, the system performs the following:

i. Creates a ledger group for each leading depreciation area of a non-leading accounting principle. This ledger group will always be assigned to the leading ledger 0L.

ii. Assigns a name to the automatically created ledger group with the naming convention "&" +number of depreciation area+" &".

Additionally, before performing this asset accounting configuration, ensure all ledger groups created are assigned to their respective accounting principles. This applies regardless of the parallel accounting approach chosen i.e. ledger approach or accounts approach.

Chart of dep. 1000 Base Line Chart of depreciation

Define Depreciation Areas

Ar.	Name of depreciation area	Real	Trgt Group	Acc.Princ.	G/L
1	Book depreciation in local currency	☑	0L	IFRS	1 Area Posts in Realtime
10	Federal Tax ACRS/MACRS	☑	0L	IFRS	0 Area Does Not Post
11	Alternative Minimum Tax	☑	0L	IFRS	0 Area Does Not Post
12	Adjusted Current Earnings	☑	0L	IFRS	0 Area Does Not Post
13	Corporate Earnings & Profits	☑	0L	IFRS	0 Area Does Not Post
30	Consolidated balance sheet in local currency	☑	LX	GAAP	1 Area Posts in Realtime
31	Consolidated balance sheet in group currency	☑	LX	GAAP	0 Area Does Not Post
32	Book depreciation in group currency	☑	0L	IFRS	0 Area Does Not Post
40	State modified ACRS	☑	0L	IFRS	0 Area Does Not Post
80	Insurance values	☑	0L	IFRS	0 Area Does Not Post

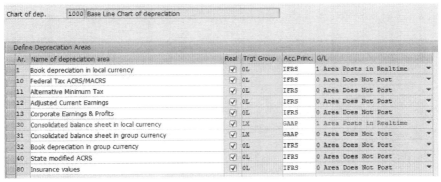

As shown in the figure, assign each depreciation to an accounting principle, as dictated by business requirements. Crucially, only the leading depreciation area of each accounting principle is set to post Acquisition and Production Costs (APC) to the GL in real-time.

If there are parallel depreciation areas that are set to post to the GL, set them to post APC periodically (similar to the classic Asset Accounting system). The exception to this is reserves for special depreciation areas, which can also post APC to the GL in real time.

Note: In the accounts approach, even though the leading valuation also posts in real time, it does not use the "Area posts in Realtime" indicator; instead, it uses the indicator "Area posts APC immediately, depreciation periodically."

4.4.3. Optional Configuration Activities in Preparation for Asset Accounting Migration

While the following customizing do not absolutely need to be performed prior to an actual migration, carefully review each one to confirm relevance to the existing migration scenario.

4.4.4. Define Depreciation Area for Quantity Update

Specify which depreciation area to use for updating quantities; otherwise, the system default of depreciation area 01 applies. This setting is especially relevant for collective low-value assets. The quantity will only be updated if a posting is made to the depreciation area.

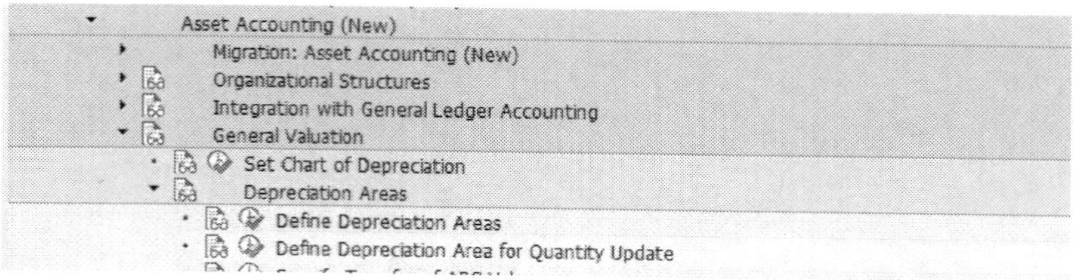
Asset Accounting (New)
Migration: Asset Accounting (New)
Organizational Structures
Integration with General Ledger Accounting
General Valuation
Set Chart of Depreciation
Depreciation Areas
Define Depreciation Areas
Define Depreciation Area for Quantity Update

4.4.5. Specify Alternative Document Type for Accounting-Principle-Specific Documents

If business requirements dictate, specify an alternative document type to override the system default for the accounting principle specific documents (valuating documents) automatically generated during an integrated asset acquisition. Note, however, that if document splitting is activated, then this setting is absolutely required, since the system cannot always pass on the document type of the entry view to the valuating documents.

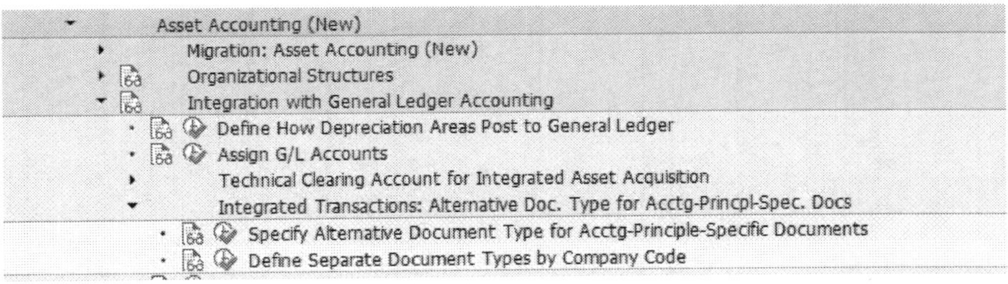
Asset Accounting (New)
Migration: Asset Accounting (New)
Organizational Structures
Integration with General Ledger Accounting
Define How Depreciation Areas Post to General Ledger
Assign G/L Accounts
Technical Clearing Account for Integrated Asset Acquisition
Integrated Transactions: Alternative Doc. Type for Acctg-Princpl-Spec. Docs
Specify Alternative Document Type for Acctg-Principle-Specific Documents
Define Separate Document Types by Company Code

4.4.6. Create Clearing Accounts for Non-Integrated Asset Acquisition

This step is only necessary if, until now, clearing accounts for the non-integrated asset acquisition were managed with open items (OI-managed). This step is not required if the accounts were not OI-managed.

In S/4HANA, it is no longer possible to clear the open items to the clearing account for non-integrated asset acquisitions – it is not possible to clear a cross-valuation document (vendor invoice) with several valuation-specific documents (capitalization of asset). The recommended approach is to create a new G/L clearing account for non-integrated asset acquisitions in the chart of accounts and in the company code, and to assign this G/L account in the account determination of Asset Accounting (Contra account Acquisition Value)

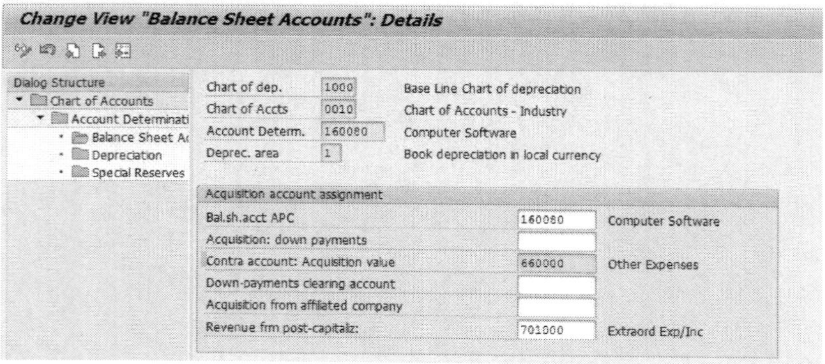
Change View "Balance Sheet Accounts": Details
Dialog Structure
Chart of Accounts
Account Determinati
Balance Sheet Ac
Depreciation
Special Reserves
Chart of dep.
1000
Base Line Chart of depreciation
Chart of Accts
0010
Chart of Accounts - Industry
Account Determ.
160080
Computer Software
Deprec. area
1
Book depreciation in local currency
Acquisition account assignment
Bal.sh.acct APC
160080
Computer Software
Acquisition: down payments
Contra account: Acquisition value
660000
Other Expenses
Down-payments clearing account
Acquisition from affiliated company
Revenue frm post-capitaliz:
701000
Extraord Exp/Inc

4.4.7. Specify Revenue Distribution for Asset Retirement

Specify at company code level how the system is to distribute revenues arising from asset retirements: either based on the net book value or on APC. In the standard system, the distribution is based on the net book value.

4.4.8. Post Net Book Value Instead of Gain/Loss

Specify at the company code level for the system to post net book value of an asset being retired to the account "Clearing of revenue from sale of assets" or "Clearing of revenue from internal sale". No profit/loss (from sale) or loss from asset retirement (after scrapping) is then posted. If this setting is not made, the standard system posts a gain or loss.

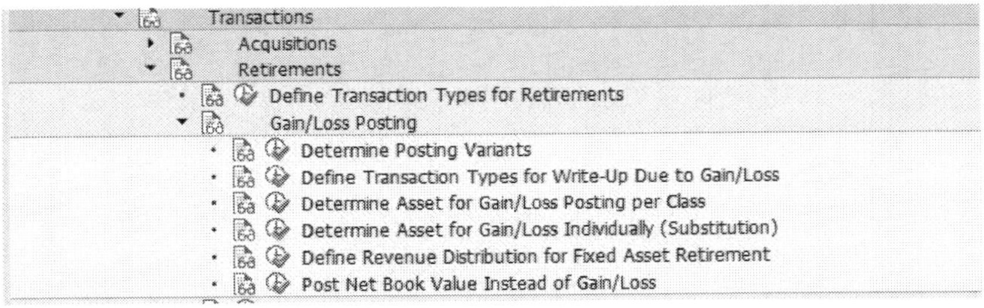
Transactions
Acquisitions
Retirements
Define Transaction Types for Retirements
Gain/Loss Posting
Determine Posting Variants
Define Transaction Types for Write-Up Due to Gain/Loss
Determine Asset for Gain/Loss Posting per Class
Determine Asset for Gain/Loss Individually (Substitution)
Define Revenue Distribution for Fixed Asset Retirement
Post Net Book Value Instead of Gain/Loss

4.4.9. Checking the Prerequisites for Activating New Asset Accounting

Use the report to check if the prerequisites for activating new Asset Accounting are met, i.e. after migrating the charts of depreciation (which are assigned to company codes) and making additional manual Customizing settings.

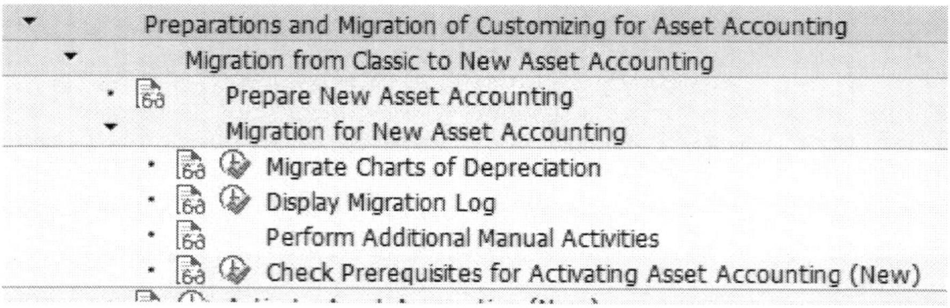
Preparations and Migration of Customizing for Asset Accounting
Migration from Classic to New Asset Accounting
Prepare New Asset Accounting
Migration for New Asset Accounting
Migrate Charts of Depreciation
Display Migration Log
Perform Additional Manual Activities
Check Prerequisites for Activating Asset Accounting (New)

The indicators from the report output must all be green; otherwise, it means activation of New Asset Accounting is not yet possible. You need to fulfill all the pre-requisite before migration.

4.4.10. Activate New Asset Accounting

Use this screen to activate asset Accounting functionality and save the setting. The system performs various checks, and only when successful does the system save the settings. New Asset Accounting is then active, and it is now possible to use the new posting logic from this point on.

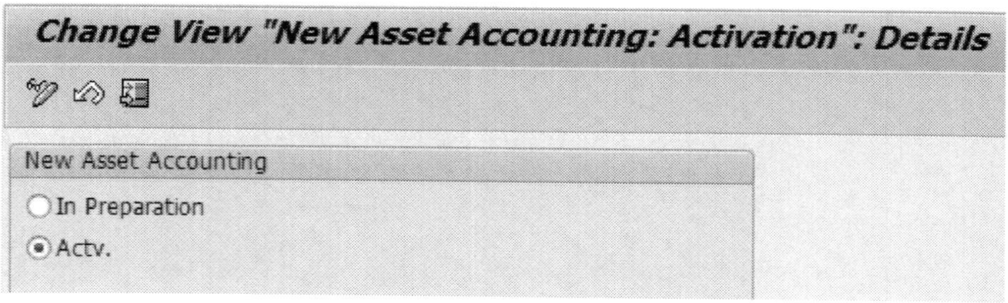
Change View "New Asset Accounting: Activation": Details
New Asset Accounting
In Preparation
Actv.

4.5. Preparations and Migration of Customizing for Controlling

In the universal journal entry (in table ACDOCA) the Controlling (CO) and Financial Accounting (FI) components are merged. Therefore, cost and revenue information is always up to date and permanently reconciled with the income statement.

The new Simplified Profitability Analysis is based on the universal journal entry as well, since all relevant account are assigned to the correct market segment characteristics in real time. Therefore, while costing-based profitability analysis is still available, and both types of profitability analysis can be used in parallel, account-based profitability analysis is still the recommended solution.

Key customizing activities that need to be executed are:

i. Execute BW-Delta Extraction for Account-Based CO-PA
ii. Delete Settings for the Change of Profitability Segment Characteristics
iii. Maintain Operating Concern
iv. Maintain Operating Concern for Banking Add-On
v. Activate Account-Based Profitability Analysis
vi. Transport Operating Concern

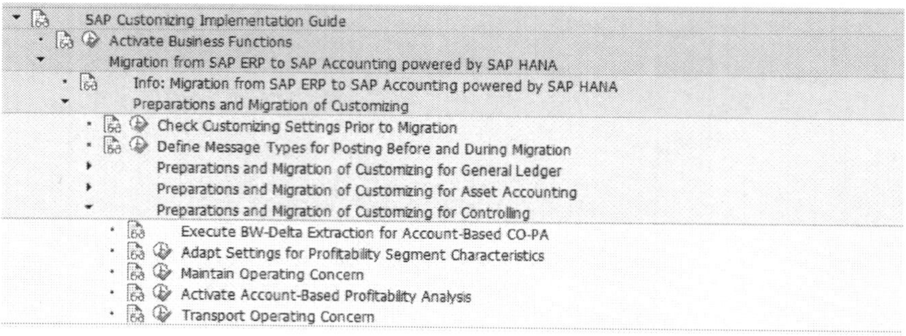
SAP Customizing Implementation Guide
Activate Business Functions
Migration from SAP ERP to SAP Accounting powered by SAP HANA
Info: Migration from SAP ERP to SAP Accounting powered by SAP HANA
Preparations and Migration of Customizing
Check Customizing Settings Prior to Migration
Define Message Types for Posting Before and During Migration
Preparations and Migration of Customizing for General Ledger
Preparations and Migration of Customizing for Asset Accounting
Preparations and Migration of Customizing for Controlling
Execute BW-Delta Extraction for Account-Based CO-PA
Adapt Settings for Profitability Segment Characteristics
Maintain Operating Concern
Activate Account-Based Profitability Analysis
Transport Operating Concern

4.5.1. Execute BW-Delta Extraction for Account-Based CO-PA

If BW is currently installed in the existing setup, perform a delta extraction for those account-based CO-PA data sources that use the delta procedure. Otherwise, account-based CO-PA line items that are not extracted before the conversion may be ignored after the conversion when the next delta is loaded.

4.5.2. Adapt Settings for Profitability Segment Characteristics

In transaction **FCO_MIG_COPA**, delete settings for profitability segment characteristics (segment level) since, going forward, each profitability segment contains all available characteristics. Summarization of specific characteristics is no longer possible and not needed, including the settings for distributed profitability analysis characteristics (segment level).

If summarization is nevertheless unavoidable due to the expected data volume, use the new summarization technique built for SAP HANA (transaction KEQ7)

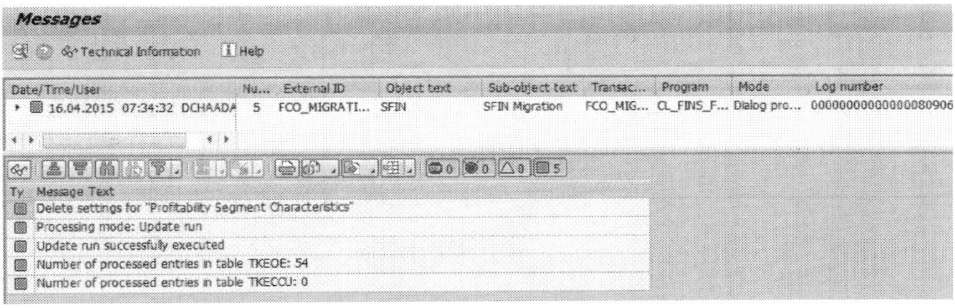
Messages
Technical Information
Help
Date/Time/User
Nu...
External ID
Object text
Sub-object text
Transac...
Program
Mode
Log number
16.04.2015 07:34:32 DCHAADA
5
FCO_MIGRATI...
SFIN
SFIN Migration
FCO_MIG...
CL_FINS_F...
Dialog pro...
00000000000000080906
Ty
Message Text
Delete settings for "Profitability Segment Characteristics"
Processing mode: Update run
Update run successfully executed
Number of processed entries in table TKEOE: 54
Number of processed entries in table TKECU: 0

4.5.3. Maintain Operating Concern

If not already done, activate Account-based Profitability Analysis for the Operating Concern using transaction KEA0. If this setting is not made, the new profitability reporting (delivered by SAP) will not be available. It is also possible to include customer-defined fields from the structure CI_COBL into the operating concern using this activity. (Note: For any changes made, always activate the data structures and generate the environment of these operating concerns.)

In case a characteristic added to the operating concern is not known to the universal journal table ACDOCA, execute the report **FCO_ADD_COPA_FIELD_TO_ACDOCA**. Activation takes some time and can only be executed in background mode. Once all errors from the action log have been resolved, the activated Operating Concern status will show green.

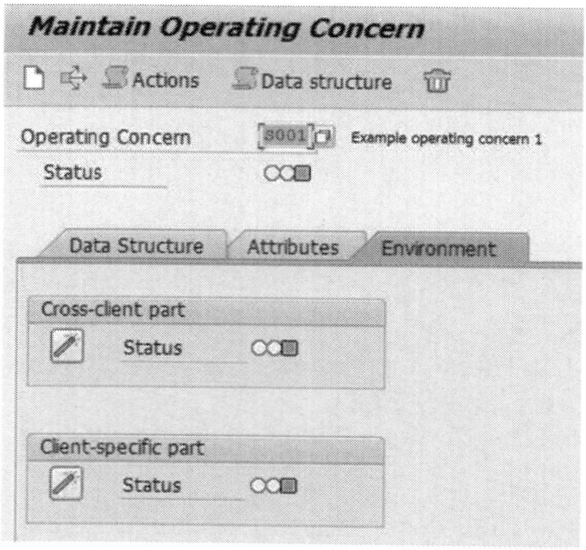
Maintain Operating Concern
Actions
Data structure
Operating Concern
8001
Example operating concern 1
Status
Data Structure
Attributes
Environment
Cross-client part
Status
Client-specific part
Status

4.5.4. Activate Account-Based Profitability Analysis

Use this utility to validate activation of Profitability Analysis per Operating Concern carried out in the previous step.

4.6. Preparatory Activities and Migration of Customizing for Credit Management

Perform the following customizing activities in preparation for Credit Management data conversion.

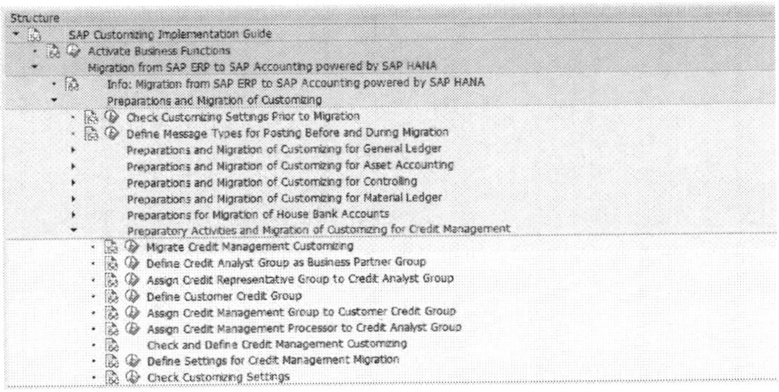
Structure
SAP Customizing Implementation Guide
Activate Business Functions
Migration from SAP ERP to SAP Accounting powered by SAP HANA
Info: Migration from SAP ERP to SAP Accounting powered by SAP HANA
Preparations and Migration of Customizing
Check Customizing Settings Prior to Migration
Define Message Types for Posting Before and During Migration
Preparations and Migration of Customizing for General Ledger
Preparations and Migration of Customizing for Asset Accounting
Preparations and Migration of Customizing for Controlling
Preparations and Migration of Customizing for Material Ledger
Preparations for Migration of House Bank Accounts
Preparatory Activities and Migration of Customizing for Credit Management
Migrate Credit Management Customizing
Define Credit Analyst Group as Business Partner Group
Assign Credit Representative Group to Credit Analyst Group
Define Customer Credit Group
Assign Credit Management Group to Customer Credit Group
Assign Credit Management Processor to Credit Analyst Group
Check and Define Credit Management Customizing
Define Settings for Credit Management Migration
Check Customizing Settings

4.6.1. Ensure Employees have been Migrated to Business Partners

Before commencing the preparation activities for credit management, ensure all employees have been migrated to business partners. Do this using the report /SHCM/RH_SYNC_BUPA_FROM_EMPL.

4.6.2. Migrate Credit Management customizing

Execute this activity to migrate the following settings to the new configuration of credit management.

i. From credit control areas to credit segments

ii. From the customizing table for the risk category to the risk class

iii. Necessary customizing entries for the documented credit decision are made

iv. Configuration settings for the automatic credit control (transaction OVA8) are set.

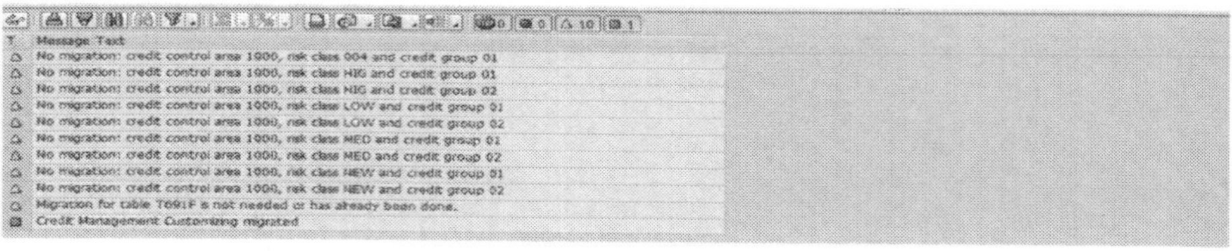
Message Text
No migration: credit control area 1000, risk class 004 and credit group 01
No migration: credit control area 1000, risk class HIG and credit group 01
No migration: credit control area 1000, risk class HIG and credit group 02
No migration: credit control area 1000, risk class LOW and credit group 01
No migration: credit control area 1000, risk class LOW and credit group 02
No migration: credit control area 1000, risk class MED and credit group 01
No migration: credit control area 1000, risk class MED and credit group 02
No migration: credit control area 1000, risk class NEW and credit group 01
No migration: credit control area 1000, risk class NEW and credit group 02
Migration for table T691F is not needed or has already been done.
Credit Management Customizing migrated

4.6.3. Define Credit Analyst Group as Business Partner Group

Define a credit analyst group as business partner of the type *group*, then in the subsequent step assign this credit analyst group to a credit representative group.

4.6.4. Define Credit Representative Group as Business Partner Relationship

In this step, define user groups per credit control area and in the second step, assign each customer to a group. The group is used as a selection criterion for the credit data list.

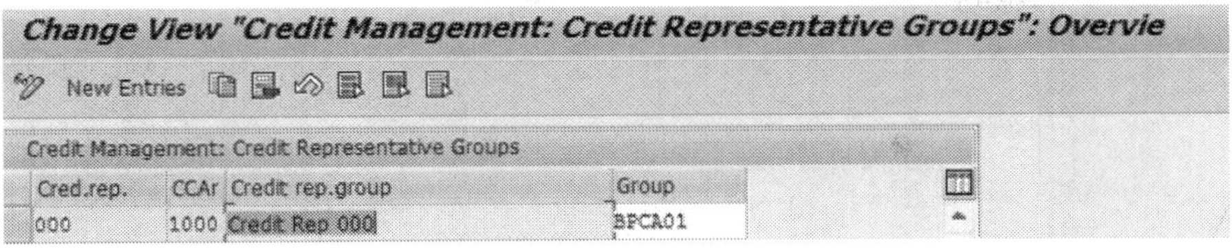
Change View "Credit Management: Credit Representative Groups": Overvie
New Entries
Credit Management: Credit Representative Groups
Cred.rep.
CCAr
Credit rep.group
Group
000
1000
Credit Rep 000
BPCA01

4.6.5. Define Customer Credit Group

Create different Customer Credit Groups based on specific business requirement and credit strategy of the firm.

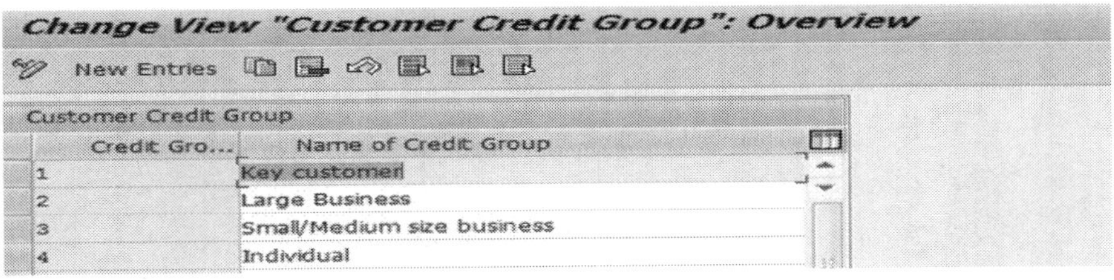
Change View "Customer Credit Group": Overview
New Entries
Customer Credit Group
Credit Gro...
Name of Credit Group
1
Key customer
2
Large Business
3
Small/Medium size business
4
Individual

4.6.6. Assign Credit Management Group to Customer Credit Group

As business requirements dictate, define groups per credit control area. In a subsequent step, assign each customer to one of these groups in the application menu for the credit management master data.

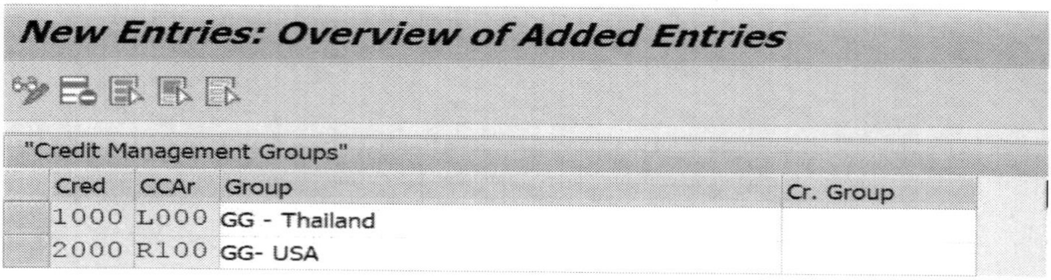
New Entries: Overview of Added Entries

"Credit Management Groups"

Cred	CCAr	Group	Cr. Group
1000	L000	GG - Thailand	
2000	R100	GG- USA	

4.6.7. Assign Credit Management Processor to Credit Analyst Group

Establish a link between Credit Management Processor (new concept in S/4HANA) and the Credit Analyst Group using relationship category UKMSBG. The credit management processor is a business partner of the type Person, to which the business partner role Employee is assigned. A prerequisite for this activity is that all employees must have been migrated to business partners.

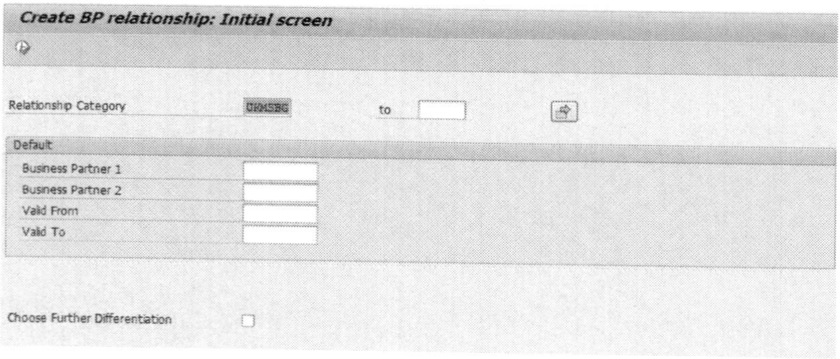
Create BP relationship: Initial screen
Relationship Category
UKMSBG
to
Default
Business Partner 1
Business Partner 2
Valid From
Valid To
Choose Further Differentiation

4.6.8. Check and Define Credit Management Customizing

Credit check types A, B and C are no longer supported in the system; therefore, if these check types have been specified anywhere, change them to check type D or leave the field blank. Execute the following checks in the SAP Reference IMG (choose Financial Supply Chain Management -> Credit Management).

i. Check the settings of Sales Documents and Delivery Documents

Change the credit check types for all sales and delivery Sales Order and Delivery Document Types to "D":

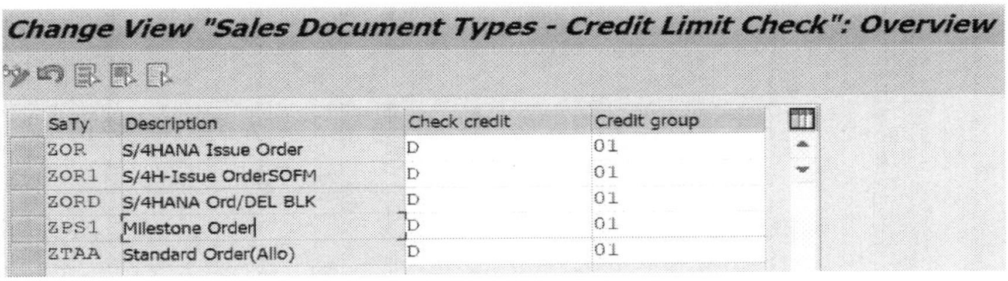
Change View "Sales Document Types - Credit Limit Check": Overview

SaTy	Description	Check credit	Credit group
ZOR	S/4HANA Issue Order	D	01
ZOR1	S/4H-Issue OrderSOFM	D	01
ZORD	S/4HANA Ord/DEL BLK	D	01
ZPS1	Milestone Order	D	01
ZTAA	Standard Order(Allo)	D	01

ii. Assign Logical System to the Element Types for Business Objects

Check whether entries for UKM_SPS_VBAK and UKM_SPS_LIKP exist and are assigned to the logical system.

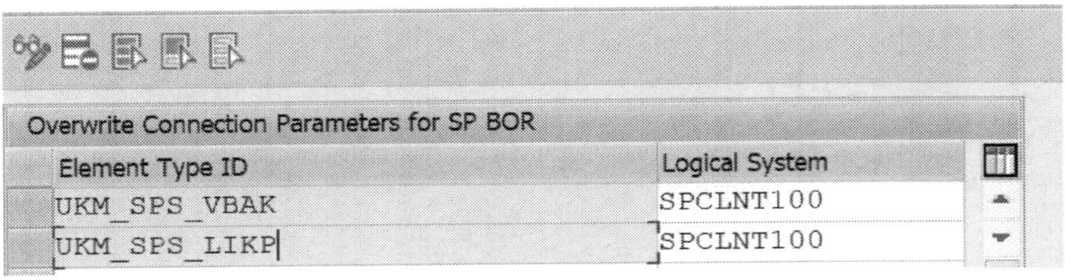
Overwrite Connection Parameters for SP BOR

Element Type ID	Logical System
UKM_SPS_VBAK	SPCLNT100
UKM_SPS_LIKP	SPCLNT100

4.6.9. Define Settings for Credit Management Migration

Specify the parameter values here for use by the system in the migration of credit management master data. These values are set by default in the business partner role or the credit limit rules, for example.

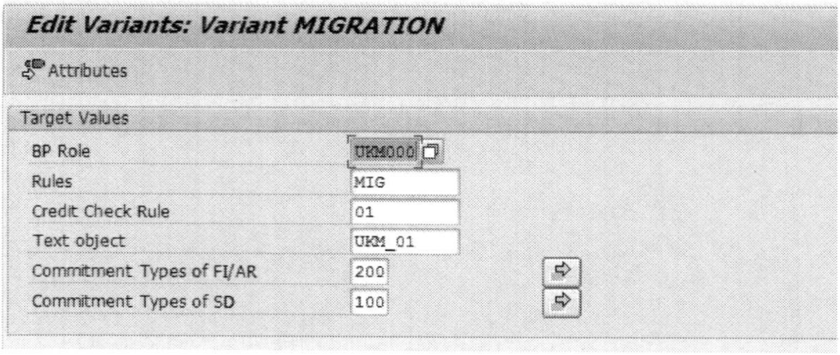
Edit Variants: Variant MIGRATION
Attributes
Target Values
BP Role
UKM000
Rules
MIG
Credit Check Rule
01
Text object
UKM_01
Commitment Types of FI/AR
200
Commitment Types of SD
100

4.6.10. Check Customizing Settings

Execute this activity for the system to check whether the credit management customizing is set up correctly for conversion. The system issues warning or error messages in case of missing or incorrect setup of customizing.

Message Text
Creditsegments checked
Risk Classes checked
DCD Settings checked
BaDI UKM_R3_ACTIVATE is active. Please read note 2196823
Default Badi Implementation UKM_R3_ACTIVATE

4.7. Preparations and Migration of Customizing for Material Ledger

Conversion to the material ledger is required in SAP HANA 1610, and this applies even if the source system is using SAP Simple Finance or migrating from a source system that's using material ledger.

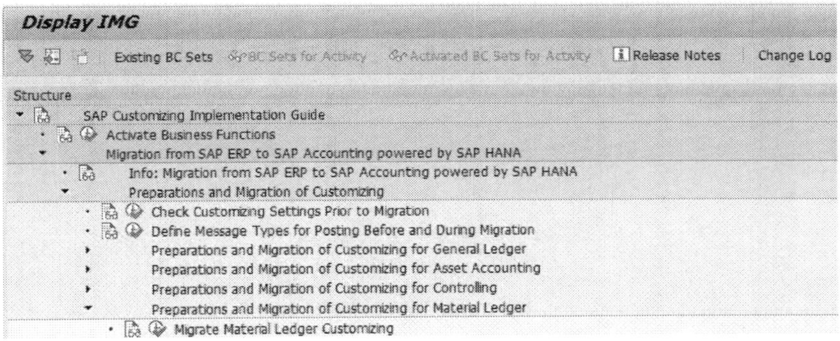
Display IMG
Existing BC Sets
BC Sets for Activity
Activated BC Sets for Activity
Release Notes
Change Log
Structure
SAP Customizing Implementation Guide
Activate Business Functions
Migration from SAP ERP to SAP Accounting powered by SAP HANA
Info: Migration from SAP ERP to SAP Accounting powered by SAP HANA
Preparations and Migration of Customizing
Check Customizing Settings Prior to Migration
Define Message Types for Posting Before and During Migration
Preparations and Migration of Customizing for General Ledger
Preparations and Migration of Customizing for Asset Accounting
Preparations and Migration of Customizing for Controlling
Preparations and Migration of Customizing for Material Ledger
Migrate Material Ledger Customizing

4.7.1. Migrate Material Ledger Customizing

Perform this activity only after the preceding preparatory activities in sections 4.1.1 through 4.6 have been completed. First execute in test mode, and, if no errors occur, execute run in update mode.

4.8. Preparatory Activities and Conversion of Customizing for Cash Management

Perform the following customizing activities in preparation for migrating Bank Account master data.

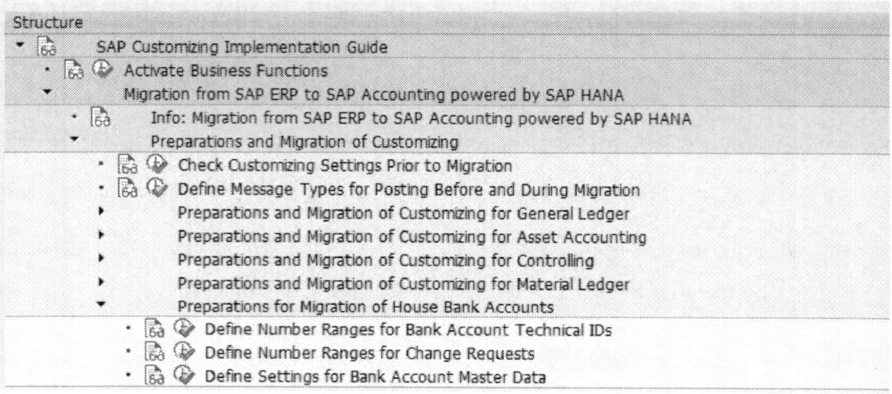
Structure
SAP Customizing Implementation Guide
Activate Business Functions
Migration from SAP ERP to SAP Accounting powered by SAP HANA
Info: Migration from SAP ERP to SAP Accounting powered by SAP HANA
Preparations and Migration of Customizing
Check Customizing Settings Prior to Migration
Define Message Types for Posting Before and During Migration
Preparations and Migration of Customizing for General Ledger
Preparations and Migration of Customizing for Asset Accounting
Preparations and Migration of Customizing for Controlling
Preparations and Migration of Customizing for Material Ledger
Preparations for Migration of House Bank Accounts
Define Number Ranges for Bank Account Technical IDs
Define Number Ranges for Change Requests
Define Settings for Bank Account Master Data

4.8.1. Define Number Ranges for Bank Account Technical IDs

Create number range intervals for bank account technical IDs. The system automatically assigns a technical ID to a bank account once it is created in the bank account master data.

4.8.2. Basic Settings for Bank Account Master Data

Define the following basic settings for the bank account master data:

i. **Assign a number range interval for bank account technical IDs**: This setting is required for the conversion of house banks. Simply apply the number range.

ii. **Assign a number range interval for bank account change request IDs**: This setting is required for the conversion of house banks. Simply apply the number range.

iii. **Define bank account types**: This setting is required for the conversion of house banks. Define different types of accounts according to business requirements, for subsequent use as an analysis dimension in reporting and planning.

iv. **Define sensitive fields to be protected for changes**: Making changes to sensitive fields defined here will trigger workflow change requests if SAP Business Workflow is enabled.

v. **Define import methods for bank statements**: The import methods defined in this screen are made available on the Additional Data tab for each bank account master record. Users can select one of defined methods as the Import Method for End-of-Day Statements, and one as the Import Method for Intra-Day Statements

vi. **Define signatory groups for payment approvals:** Define different groups of authorized signatories to suit different business purposes.

vii. **Define the signatory groups and the approval sequence for approval patterns:** Define two types of approval patterns for payments: sequential and non-sequential.

viii. **Assign approval patterns to company codes and account types**, and specify the approval pattern priority: The approval patterns are activated at the level of assigned company codes and account type.

5. Data Conversion to S/4HANA 1610

5.1. Partitioning of the Universal Journal Entry Line Items Table (ACDOCA)

As a result of conversion activities, the ACDOCA table is filled from the areas of G/L, controlling, material ledger, and asset accounting, and, depending on the data volume in the source applications, is highly susceptible to a high number of records. This can have a negative effect on performance of selects and merge operations.

As a pre-conversion activity, the technical team should consider partitioning the data to prevent the negative effects mentioned above. Partitioning splits tables horizontally into disjunctive sub-tables or partitions. In this way, large tables are broken down into smaller, more manageable units.

5.2. Regenerate Core Data Services (CDS) Views and Field Mapping

Before using CDS to define the objects in the System, BASIS team (with S_DEVELOP authorization) should perform the following required activities:

i. **Execute** the activities from: SPRO-> Migration from SAP ERP to SAP Accounting powered by SAP HANA - > Migration -> Regenerate CDS Views and Field Mapping.

ii. Regenerate the compatibility and data migration views so as to adapt them to the configuration of customer-specific entities.

iii. Generate the redirection of SELECT-statements from the concerned data base tables to the corresponding compatibility views.

iv. Regenerate the mapping of customer-specific fields in the data conversion procedure.

As the figure below demonstrates, errors may occur during the activation process. This kind of error can be solved by resetting the CDS views as described in the SAP Note 1987083. This note references executing the report "FINS_MIGRATION_STATUS".

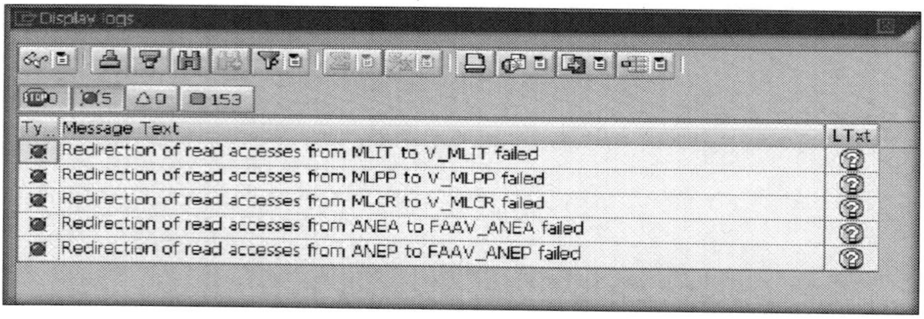
Display logs
5
0
153
Ty..
Message Text
LTxt
Redirection of read accesses from MLIT to V_MLIT failed
Redirection of read accesses from MLPP to V_MLPP failed
Redirection of read accesses from MLCR to V_MLCR failed
Redirection of read accesses from ANEA to FAAV_ANEA failed
Redirection of read accesses from ANEP to FAAV_ANEP failed

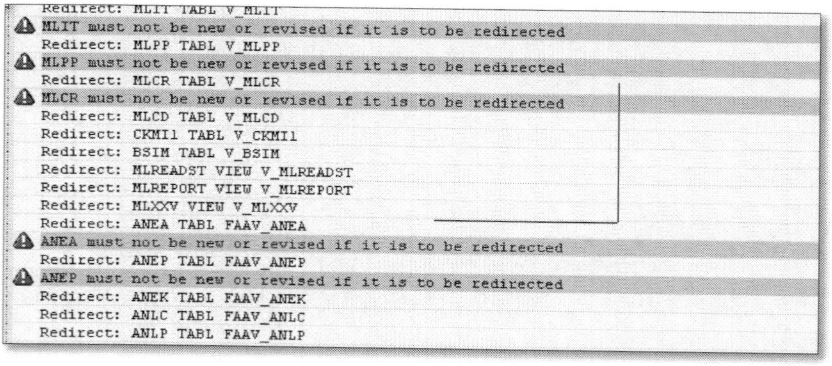
Redirect: MLIT TABL V_MLIT
MLIT must not be new or revised if it is to be redirected
Redirect: MLPP TABL V_MLPP
MLPP must not be new or revised if it is to be redirected
Redirect: MLCR TABL V_MLCR
MLCR must not be new or revised if it is to be redirected
Redirect: MLCD TABL V_MLCD
Redirect: CKMI1 TABL V_CKMI1
Redirect: BSIM TABL V_BSIM
Redirect: MLREADST VIEW V_MLREADST
Redirect: MLREPORT VIEW V_MLREPORT
Redirect: MLXXV VIEW V_MLXXV
Redirect: ANEA TABL FAAV_ANEA
ANEA must not be new or revised if it is to be redirected
Redirect: ANEP TABL FAAV_ANEP
ANEP must not be new or revised if it is to be redirected
Redirect: ANEK TABL FAAV_ANEK
Redirect: ANLC TABL FAAV_ANLC
Redirect: ANLP TABL FAAV_ANLP

5.3. Migration of Cost Elements and Customizing

In the new system, Cost Elements are no longer maintained separately in CO, but are managed as a special type of G/L account. Since the Controlling (CO) and Financial Accounting (FI) components have been merged, and as this makes secondary cost elements in classic CO obsolete, perform all activities under the section **Migration of Cost Elements and Customizing** to migrate Cost Element related data to the new structure.

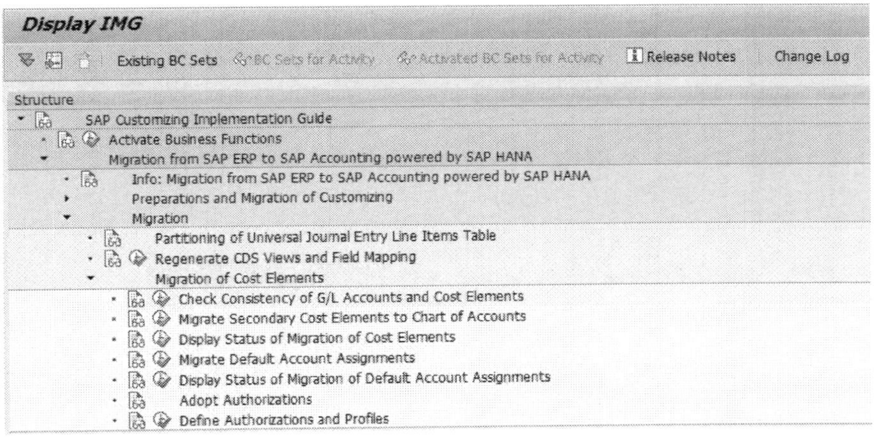
Display IMG
Existing BC Sets
BC Sets for Activity
Activated BC Sets for Activity
Release Notes
Change Log
Structure
SAP Customizing Implementation Guide
Activate Business Functions
Migration from SAP ERP to SAP Accounting powered by SAP HANA
Info: Migration from SAP ERP to SAP Accounting powered by SAP HANA
Preparations and Migration of Customizing
Migration
Partitioning of Universal Journal Entry Line Items Table
Regenerate CDS Views and Field Mapping
Migration of Cost Elements
Check Consistency of G/L Accounts and Cost Elements
Migrate Secondary Cost Elements to Chart of Accounts
Display Status of Migration of Cost Elements
Migrate Default Account Assignments
Display Status of Migration of Default Account Assignments
Adopt Authorizations
Define Authorizations and Profiles

5.3.1. Check Consistency of G/L Accounts and Cost Elements

Use this report to check whether the G/L accounts and cost elements are consistent with each other. An inconsistency could be, for example, that no G/L account exists for a primary cost element.

If this occurs, correct the indicated inconsistencies; otherwise, the G/L account master records will have the wrong account types after conversion.

If errors occur as indicated below, confirm whether the accounts listed are primary cost elements and, if true, that the cost element is a primary cost element. If both checks are positive, then change the setting of these cost elements or GL account in transaction FS00. In transaction FS00, change the existing Account Type to "Primary Costs or Revenue" and choose "P&L Statement Accounts" as the Account Group. Once corrected, re-run the check to confirm resolution.

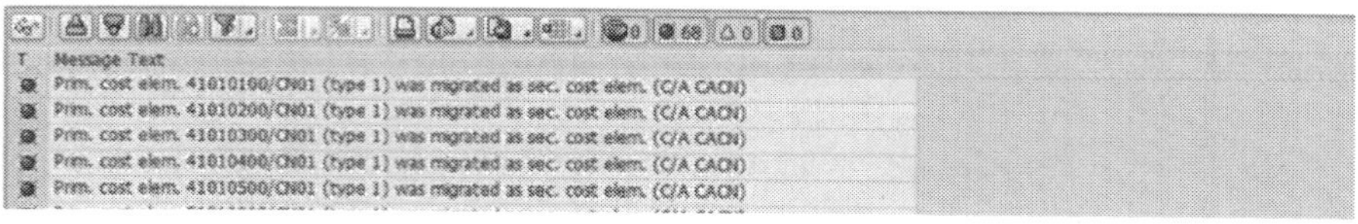
Message Text
Prim. cost elem. 41010100/CN01 (type 1) was migrated as sec. cost elem. (C/A CACN)
Prim. cost elem. 41010200/CN01 (type 1) was migrated as sec. cost elem. (C/A CACN)
Prim. cost elem. 41010300/CN01 (type 1) was migrated as sec. cost elem. (C/A CACN)
Prim. cost elem. 41010400/CN01 (type 1) was migrated as sec. cost elem. (C/A CACN)
Prim. cost elem. 41010500/CN01 (type 1) was migrated as sec. cost elem. (C/A CACN)

5.3.2. Migrate Secondary Cost Elements to Chart of Accounts

Since all cost elements are now managed as G/L accounts, execute the migration utility (transaction FINS_MIG_GCM) to migrate all secondary cost elements. After the merge, both primary and secondary cost elements are represented as G/L accounts. A new database field, type of a general ledger account (GLACCOUNT_TYPE), is populated.

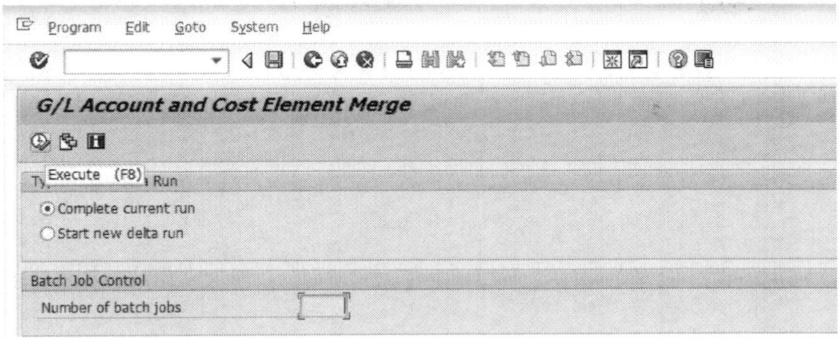
Program Edit Goto System Help
G/L Account and Cost Element Merge
Execute (F8)
Run
Complete current run
Start new delta run
Batch Job Control
Number of batch jobs

5.3.3. Display Status of Migration of Cost Elements

Monitor the status of conversion of the secondary cost element conversion (transaction FINS_MIG_MONITOR_GCM).

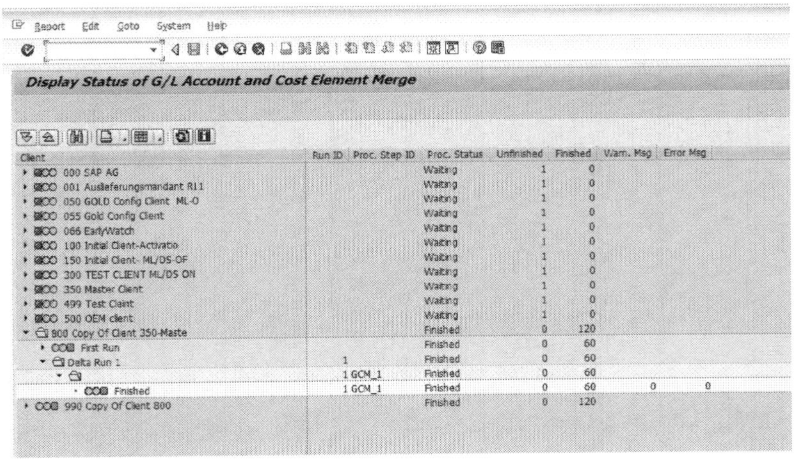
Report Edit Goto System Help
Display Status of G/L Account and Cost Element Merge
Client
Run ID
Proc. Step ID
Proc. Status
Unfinished
Finished
Warn. Msg
Error Msg
000 SAP AG
001 Auslieferungsmandant R11
050 GOLD Config Client ML-O
055 Gold Config Client
066 EarlyWatch
100 Initial Client-Activatio
150 Initial Client- ML/DS-OF
300 TEST CLIENT ML/DS ON
350 Master Client
499 Test Client
500 OEM client
800 Copy Of Client 350-Maste
First Run
Delta Run 1
1 GCM_1
Finished
990 Copy Of Client 800
Waiting
Finished

5.3.4. Migrate Default Account Assignments

With the conversion of cost elements to the chart of accounts, all the required fields from cost element master data, with the exception of the default account assignment, are moved to the GL account maintenance screen. Execute this utility to move the default account assignment from the master data table to customization table TKAA (transaction OKB9).

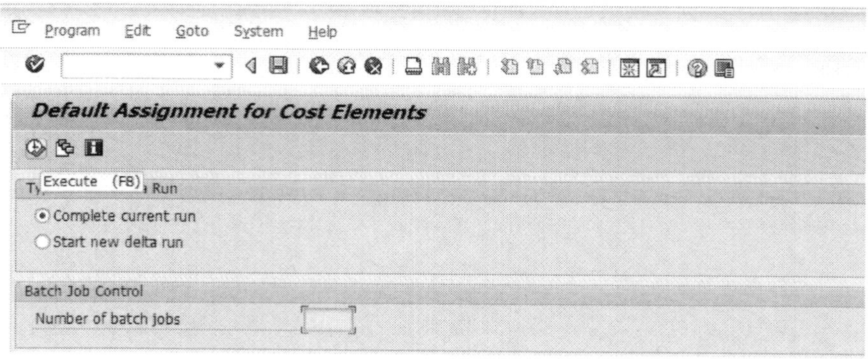
Program
Edit
Goto
System
Help
Default Assignment for Cost Elements
Execute (F8)
Run
Complete current run
Start new delta run
Batch Job Control
Number of batch jobs

5.3.5. Display Status of Migration of Default Account Assignments

Once the above step has completed, execute the utility "Display Status of Conversion of Default Account Assignments" to see if the conversion has been completed successfully. Analyze any errors as shown below:

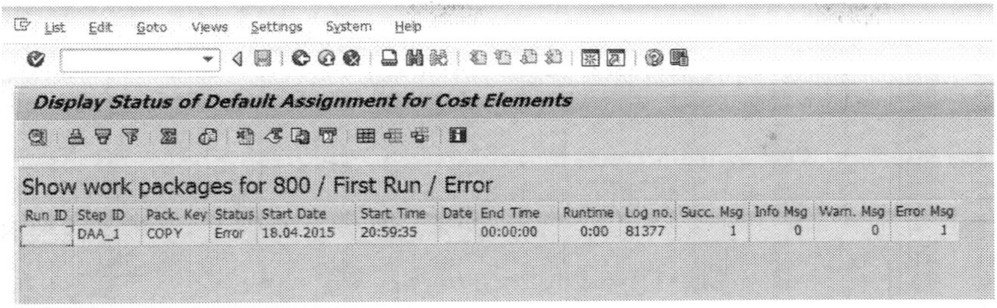
List Edit Goto Views Settings System Help
Display Status of Default Assignment for Cost Elements
Show work packages for 800 / First Run / Error
Run ID Step ID Pack. Key Status Start Date Start Time Date End Time Runtime Log no. Succ. Msg Info Msg Warn. Msg Error Msg
DAA_1 COPY Error 18.04.2015 20:59:35 00:00:00 0:00 81377 1 0 0 1

Upon double click on the "message no.", the system displays the screen as below.

Note: It may be necessary to rerun the program again for conversion to be completely successful.

Message Text
LTxt
Default assignment for cost elements in controlling area COPY
Default Account Assi step DAA_1 failed for work package COPY; try again

5.3.6. Adapt Authorizations

The merge of cost elements and G/L accounts requires adjustments to authorizations for creating cost elements. Use transaction PFCG to grant additional authorization to create or change cost element master data and/or maintain accounts of the account type Secondary Costs.

5.4. Technical Check of Transaction Data

After installation of S/4HANA 1610 system, use the activities under the section **Technical Check of Transaction Data** step to check whether all FI documents are complete and correct, and to identify and correct inconsistent documents in the system before starting the data conversion process.

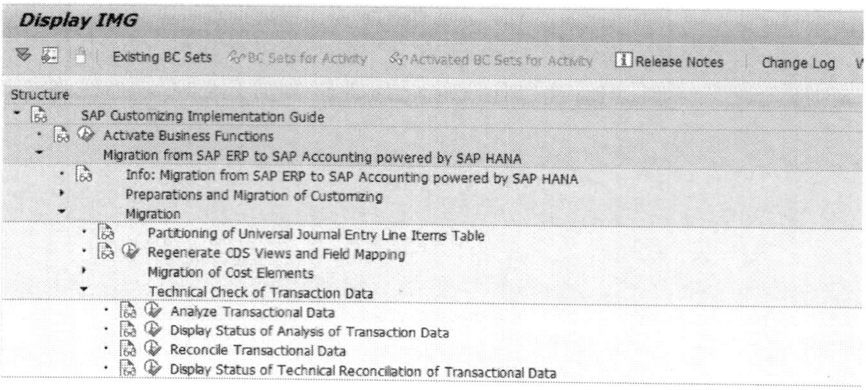
Display IMG
Existing BC Sets
BC Sets for Activity
Activated BC Sets for Activity
Release Notes
Change Log
Structure
SAP Customizing Implementation Guide
Activate Business Functions
Migration from SAP ERP to SAP Accounting powered by SAP HANA
Info: Migration from SAP ERP to SAP Accounting powered by SAP HANA
Preparations and Migration of Customizing
Migration
Partitioning of Universal Journal Entry Line Items Table
Regenerate CDS Views and Field Mapping
Migration of Cost Elements
Technical Check of Transaction Data
Analyze Transactional Data
Display Status of Analysis of Transaction Data
Reconcile Transactional Data
Display Status of Technical Reconciliation of Transactional Data

5.4.1. Analyze Transactional Data

Execute this step in all clients, even if there is no transactional data. The following checks are performed by the system:

i. Zero-Balance check
ii. Check if all document line items have a document
iii. Check if line items are missing
iv. Check if clearing information is missing
v. Check if entries are missing in backup-index tables or if duplicate entries exist in backup index tables

vi. Check if information about archiving or partially archived documents is missing in backup tables of indices

vii. Check if the clearing specific to ledger groups field is valid in line item table

viii. Check if all currency information of the documents matches the currency customizing

ix. Check if open item management flag of master and transactional data are identical

x. Check if the document date of the document header is a valid date

5.4.2. Display Status of Analysis of Transaction Data

Once the above activity is executed for analyzing the transactional data, ensure that there is no error by executing the utility for checking the status of the analysis.

If there is any error, the conversion process must be stopped and error corrected before proceeding further.

5.4.3. Reconcile Transactional Data

Execute this utility to check that the FI documents are consistent and ready to be migrated. The program reconciles the existing transactional data to ensure that the data conversion is executed correctly. It checks necessary prerequisites for the programs (like having a document header per line item which is needed for the corresponding link to work properly) and it checks that both parts of a set of redundant data (like documents and application indices) are consistent. **Note:** Make sure every inconsistency is resolved before starting the data conversion.

The following checks are applied:

i. GL Document:

   1. The following fields of the document header are filled: WAERS
   2. Existence of line items to each header (depending on document type) and vice versa
   3. Every document has a zero balance

ii. New GL Document (only applied if already active)

   1. Existence of New GL line items per BSEG and vice versa
   2. Same amount, if aggregated to BSEG level (BUZEI)
   3. Every document has balance zero based on the New GL line items
   4. Same value of certain attributes: BUDAT, RACCT, RWCUR

iii. FI-GL/AP/AR Application Indices

   1. Existence of an index entry per document line and vice versa (if required)

2. Equality of most important fields (BUKRS, BELNR, GJAHR, BUZEI, BUDAT, BLDAT, DMBTR, SAKNR, HKONT, LIFNR, KUNNR)
3. Flag, whether corresponding document of an application index entry is already archived (XARCH), is set correctly
4. The original content of the application Indices is saved in tables with _BCK as prefix.

iv. CO Document

1. Existence of document header per line item
2. Reconciliation of aggregates and line items is done in separate reports
3. Reconciliation of asset management is done in separate reports
4. Reconciliation of material ledger management is not done on item level, as only balances are migrated

5.4.4. Display Status of Technical Reconciliation of Transactional Data

Run this tool to display the status of the technical reconciliation of transactional data. The program displays a list of all clients for which data processing is performed. For each client, it includes the processed data packages and their processing status. The data packages are specified using their technical names, which can consist, for example, of a company code, ledger ID, year, and period. If mass data processing has not been performed for a client, the processing status of the client is marked with a red traffic light.

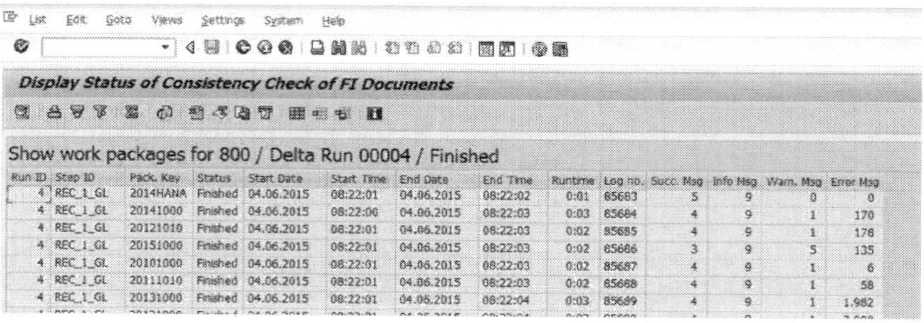
List Edit Goto Views Settings System Help
Display Status of Consistency Check of FI Documents
Show work packages for 800 / Delta Run 00004 / Finished
Run ID Step ID Pack. Key Status Start Date Start Time End Date End Time Runtime Log no. Succ. Msg Info Msg Warn. Msg Error Msg
4 REC_1_GL 2014HANA Finished 04.06.2015 08:22:01 04.06.2015 08:22:02 0:01 85683 5 9 0 0
4 REC_1_GL 20141000 Finished 04.06.2015 08:22:00 04.06.2015 08:22:03 0:03 85684 4 9 1 170
4 REC_1_GL 20121010 Finished 04.06.2015 08:22:01 04.06.2015 08:22:03 0:02 85685 4 9 1 178
4 REC_1_GL 20151000 Finished 04.06.2015 08:22:01 04.06.2015 08:22:03 0:02 85686 3 9 5 135
4 REC_1_GL 20101000 Finished 04.06.2015 08:22:01 04.06.2015 08:22:03 0:02 85687 4 9 1 6
4 REC_1_GL 20111010 Finished 04.06.2015 08:22:01 04.06.2015 08:22:03 0:02 85688 4 9 1 58
4 REC_1_GL 20131000 Finished 04.06.2015 08:22:01 04.06.2015 08:22:04 0:03 85689 4 9 1 1.982

5.5. Material Ledger Migration

Execute the following IMG activities to migrate material ledger data to the universal journal.

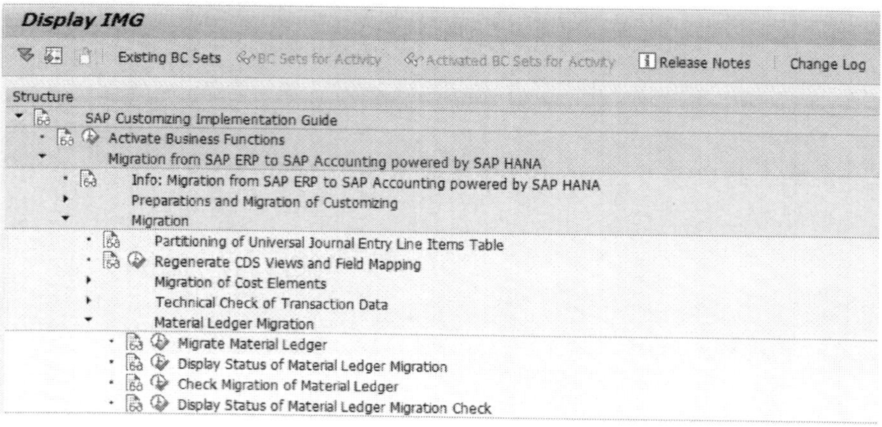
Display IMG
Existing BC Sets
BC Sets for Activity
Activated BC Sets for Activity
Release Notes
Change Log
Structure
SAP Customizing Implementation Guide
Activate Business Functions
Migration from SAP ERP to SAP Accounting powered by SAP HANA
Info: Migration from SAP ERP to SAP Accounting powered by SAP HANA
Preparations and Migration of Customizing
Migration
Partitioning of Universal Journal Entry Line Items Table
Regenerate CDS Views and Field Mapping
Migration of Cost Elements
Technical Check of Transaction Data
Material Ledger Migration
Migrate Material Ledger
Display Status of Material Ledger Migration
Check Migration of Material Ledger
Display Status of Material Ledger Migration Check

5.5.1. Migrate Material Ledger

Run this utility to activate the material ledger for all valuation areas. This creates material ledger master data and converts inventory values and material prices into the material ledger currencies (local, group, and an additional currency). In addition, production and purchase order history entries are converted into group currency and an additional currency.

If the material ledger is already active in the source system for all valuation areas, post-conversion takes place. In post-conversion, missing history table entries (tables EBEWH, MBEWH, QBEWH and OBEWH) are migrated to the material ledger, and any material ledger inconsistencies are resolved. Note: If there are outstanding issues encountered with history table MBEWH, review and where applicable implement SAP Notes **2270876** and **2135878**.

5.5.2. Display Status of Material Ledger Migration

Execute this utility to check the current status of material ledger conversion. The figure below shows the output of the program where conversion occurred as expected – conversion is successful if one of the following information statuses is shown for all valuation areas in the client:

- ✓ ML live since S/4 HANA conversion

- ✓ ML live before S/4HANA conversion and post-conversion took place

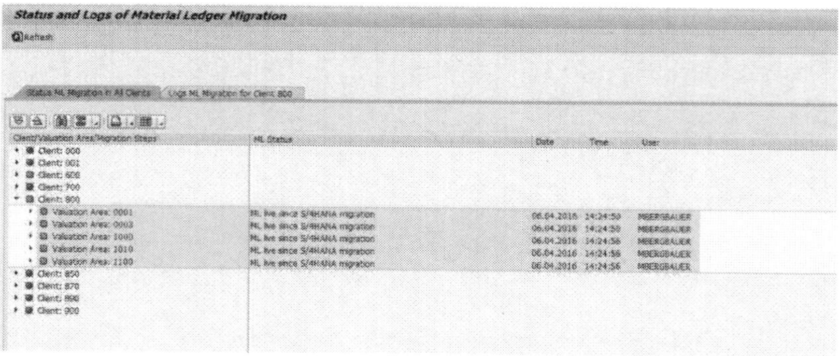
Status and Logs of Material Ledger Migration
Refresh
Client/Valuation Area/Migration Steps
ML Status
Date
Time
User
Client: 000
Client: 700
Valuation Area: 0001
ML live since S/4HANA migration
06.04.2016
MBERGBAUER
Client: 850
Client: 900

Material ledger conversion is still in process if the following status is shown:

- × ML not live
- × ML live before S/4HANA conversion. However, post-conversion missing

5.5.3. Check Migration of Material Ledger

Perform this activity after the Migrate Material Ledger activity has been completed successfully and only after all valuation areas are deemed active in the client by the Display Status of Material Ledger Conversion activity (see figure above). The system checks whether the material ledger is active in all valuation areas and performs various the technical checks listed below:

i. Any master records which do not have a corresponding MARA table entry
ii. Any mother segments as part of split valuation that do not have an entry in table CKMLPR
iii. Any records for which the MLMAA flag was not set properly
iv. Any cases where the record and the corresponding field values are not the same in the old and new xBEW(H) table
v. Any production order histories that were not converted into the required currencies

Any failure in the above checks is an indication that Material Ledger data conversion has not occurred in a consistent fashion, and the system therefore returns an error. Pursue errors by researching SAP Notes and/or raising a message with SAP support.

5.5.4. Display Status of Material Ledger Migration Check

Display the results of the Check Conversion of Material Ledger activity carried out in the previous step.

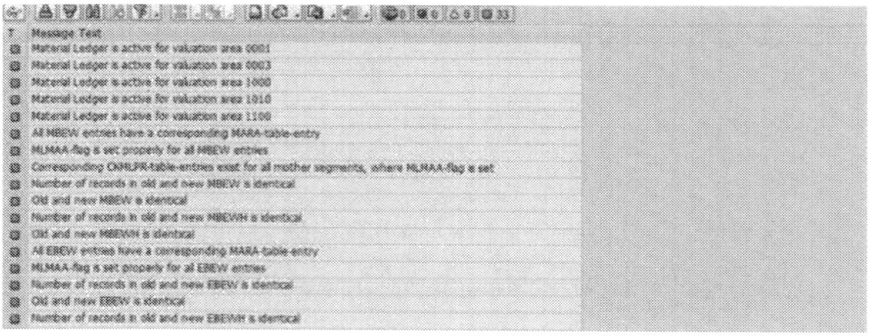
Message Text
Material Ledger is active for valuation area 0001
Material Ledger is active for valuation area 0003
Material Ledger is active for valuation area 1000
Material Ledger is active for valuation area 1010
Material Ledger is active for valuation area 1100
All MBEW entries have a corresponding MARA-table-entry
MLMAA-flag is set properly for all MBEW entries
Corresponding CKMLPR-table-entries exist for all mother segments, where MLMAA-flag is set
Number of records in old and new MBEW is identical
Old and new MBEW is identical
Number of records in old and new MBEWH is identical
Old and new MBEWH is identical
All EBEW entries have a corresponding MARA-table-entry
MLMAA-flag is set properly for all EBEW entries
Number of records in old and new EBEW is identical
Old and new EBEW is identical
Number of records in old and new EBEWH is identical

5.6. Enrichment of Transactional Data

Perform the steps in this customization activity to enrich transactional data and migrate into S/4HANA Finance 1610.

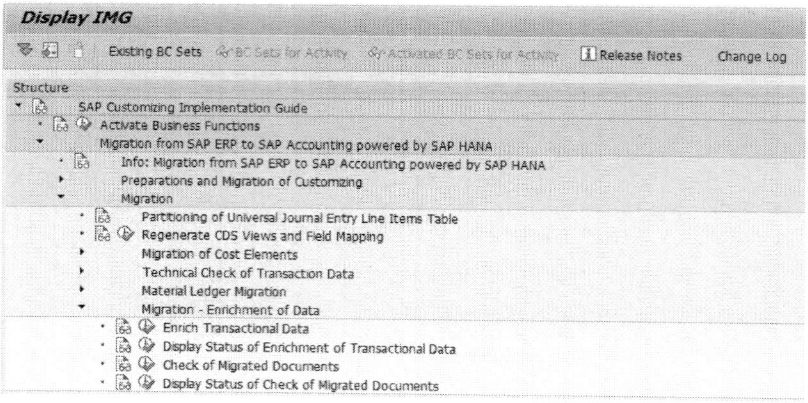
Display IMG
Existing BC Sets
BC Sets for Activity
Activated BC Sets for Activity
Release Notes
Change Log
Structure
SAP Customizing Implementation Guide
Activate Business Functions
Migration from SAP ERP to SAP Accounting powered by SAP HANA
Info: Migration from SAP ERP to SAP Accounting powered by SAP HANA
Preparations and Migration of Customizing
Migration
Partitioning of Universal Journal Entry Line Items Table
Regenerate CDS Views and Field Mapping
Migration of Cost Elements
Technical Check of Transaction Data
Material Ledger Migration
Migration - Enrichment of Data
Enrich Transactional Data
Display Status of Enrichment of Transactional Data
Check of Migrated Documents
Display Status of Check of Migrated Documents

5.6.1. Execute the activity Enrich Transactional Data

Execute this utility in all clients to enrich transaction data and documents before conversion to the new data structure.

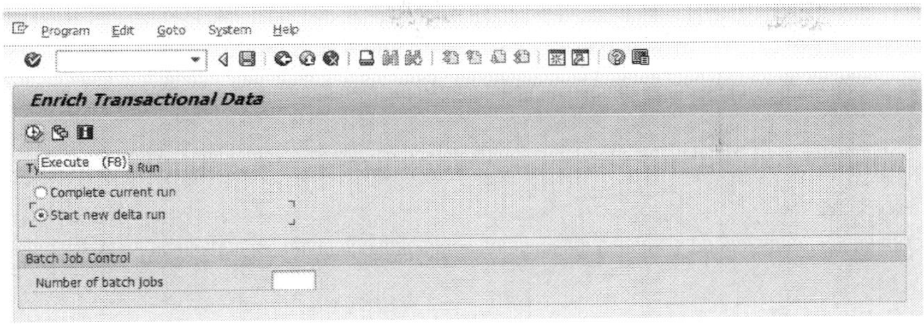
Program Edit Goto System Help
Enrich Transactional Data
Execute (F8)
Run
Complete current run
Start new delta run
Batch Job Control
Number of batch jobs

The program performs the following actions:

i. Fills BSEG-fields from BKPF
ii. Fills COEP from COBK and OBJNR
iii. Fills profit center fields into CO line items
iv. Fills company code data into old CO line items
v. Fills company code data into old CO totals
vi. Fills BSEG_ADD from FAGLBSIS/AS
vii. Fills COSP_BAK-BUKRS and COSS_BAK-BUKRS

5.6.2. Display Status of Enrichment of Transactional Data

Execute this utility to display the status of the enrichment of transactional data for all clients for which data processing is performed.

5.6.3. Check of Migrated Documents

Execute this step after enriching the transactional data as described above, as it checks fields which are used in the next conversion steps. Execute the utility in all clients irrespective of whether they have transactional data so that the conversion program can set the status of this client to "Finished". If the check results in errors, check and correct the reason for this conversion failure, then repeat the conversion check.

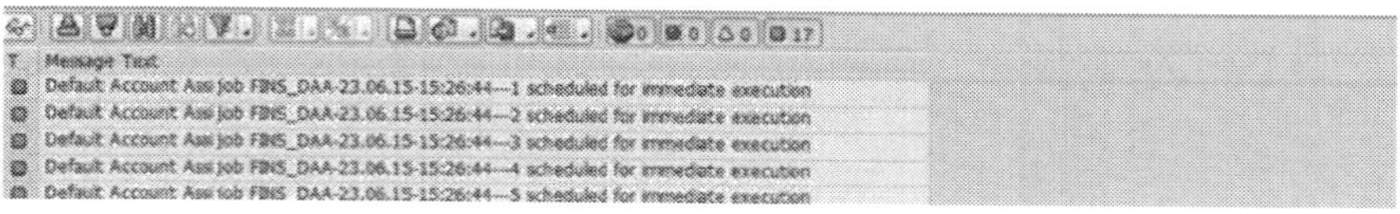
Message Text
Default Account Ass job FINS_DAA-23.06.15-15:26:44---1 scheduled for immediate execution
Default Account Ass job FINS_DAA-23.06.15-15:26:44---2 scheduled for immediate execution
Default Account Ass job FINS_DAA-23.06.15-15:26:44---3 scheduled for immediate execution
Default Account Ass job FINS_DAA-23.06.15-15:26:44---4 scheduled for immediate execution
Default Account Ass job FINS_DAA-23.06.15-15:26:44---5 scheduled for immediate execution

5.6.4. Display Status of Check of Migrated Documents.

Display the status of the check of the documents conversion in all clients for which data processing is performed.

5.7. Migration of Line Items into New Data Structure

Once the data enrichment activity is complete, execute the customizing activities under the section **Conversion of Line Items into New Data Structure** to migrate documents and line items to the data structure.

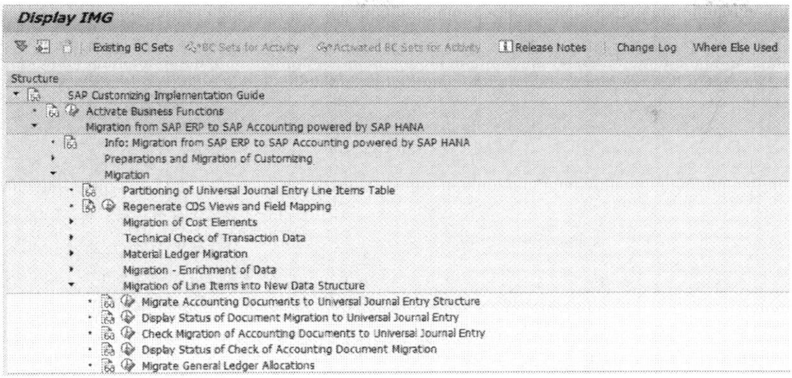
Display IMG
Existing BC Sets
BC Sets for Activity
Activated BC Sets for Activity
Release Notes
Change Log
Where Else Used
Structure
SAP Customizing Implementation Guide
Activate Business Functions
Migration from SAP ERP to SAP Accounting powered by SAP HANA
Info: Migration from SAP ERP to SAP Accounting powered by SAP HANA
Preparations and Migration of Customizing
Migration
Partitioning of Universal Journal Entry Line Items Table
Regenerate CDS Views and Field Mapping
Migration of Cost Elements
Technical Check of Transaction Data
Material Ledger Migration
Migration - Enrichment of Data
Migration of Line Items into New Data Structure
Migrate Accounting Documents to Universal Journal Entry Structure
Display Status of Document Migration to Universal Journal Entry
Check Migration of Accounting Documents to Universal Journal Entry
Display Status of Check of Accounting Document Migration
Migrate General Ledger Allocations

Perform the steps below in all clients in the SAP system, if the source system is using classic Asset Accounting, new Asset Accounting, classic General Ledger Accounting, new General Ledger Accounting, or the SAP Simple Finance add-on.

5.7.1. Migrate Accounting Documents to Universal Journal Entry Structure

Execute this utility to allow the system to populate the universal journal entry (UJE) by combining the transactional data of the applications FI, FI-GL, CO and FI-AA. Additionally, the characteristics of account-based CO-PA are added to UJE items, which are assigned to a profitability segment.

Ensure conversion take places in all clients of the SAP system, including clients that have no transactional data so that the conversion program can set the status of this client to "Finished." **If**

the checks results in errors, correct them and then restart the conversion.

5.7.2. Display Status of Document Migration to Universal Journal Entry

Execute this utility once the previous step has completed without errors and ensure the program returns error free status (green traffic light) as shown below.

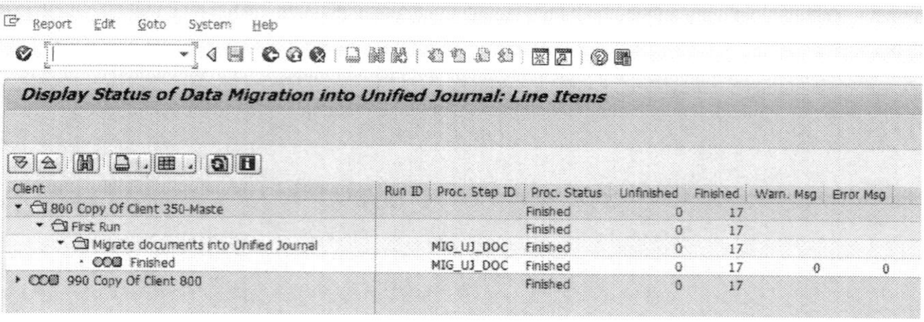
Report Edit Goto System Help
Display Status of Data Migration into Unified Journal: Line Items
Client
Run ID
Proc. Step ID
Proc. Status
Unfinished
Finished
Warn. Msg
Error Msg
800 Copy Of Client 350-Maste
First Run
Migrate documents into Unified Journal
Finished
990 Copy Of Client 800
MIG_UJ_DOC
Finished
0
17
0
0

5.7.3. Check Migration of Accounting Documents to Universal Journal Entry

Execute this reconciliation step in all clients after the conversion to ACDOCA step, to ensure all accounting documents have been migrated correctly to the Universal Journal Entry (UJE) structure. In every case the system checks for:

i. Existence on the granularity of the compatibility view which might aggregate some lines of ACDOCA

ii. Equality of some amount fields (aggregated to the level of the compatibility view) -- some amounts are taken from ML and CO with a tolerance of 0.1% for rounding differences
iii. Equality for further important fields (including clearing information)

In case of New GL Line Items, CO-line items, and AA-line items, the compatibility view, which reproduces the original line item table, is compared to the original values. In case of BSEG, no compatibility view exists, and the check is executed directly.

The following former line items tables are considered for the check:

i. New GL Line Item tables (like FAGLFLEXA) including Industry and Customer tables
ii. Cost Totals for External Postings (COSP)
iii. Costs Totals for Internal Postings (COSS)
iv. Document Header (ANEK) and Line Items (ANEP) for Asset Management

In addition, there are consistency checks for ACDOCA:

i. No duplicate entry (this is necessary as ACDOCA is not delivered with a primary key such that the DB ensures this)
ii. Balance zero for document with line items from FI-GL (CO does not guarantee balance zero)

This step must be completed before conversion of balances, since the balances will be calculated from the line items.

5.7.4. Display Status of Check of Accounting Document Migration

Check the status of the accounting document conversion and do not proceed to the next conversion step until all errors are resolved.

5.7.5. Migrate General Ledger Allocations

Run this program to change the existing G/L allocation cycles for actual values to new journal entry database tables. More specifically, all G/L allocation cycles that refer to the Flexible General Ledger summary table FAGLFLEXT are changed to the new view ACDOCT. In addition, all field usage definitions for fields of FAGLFLEXT are copied to new entries for the same fields of ACDOCT.

Run the program as a test run with extended checks and have the log displayed.

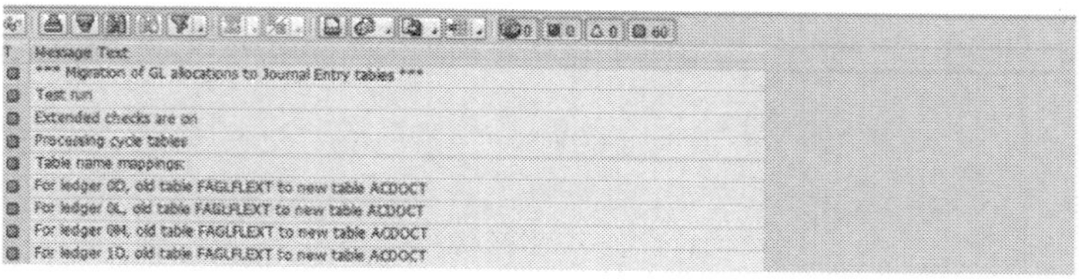
Message Text
*** Migration of GL allocations to Journal Entry tables ***
Test run
Extended checks are on
Processing cycle tables
Table name mappings:
For ledger 0D, old table FAGLFLEXT to new table ACDOCT
For ledger 0L, old table FAGLFLEXT to new table ACDOCT
For ledger 0M, old table FAGLFLEXT to new table ACDOCT
For ledger 1D, old table FAGLFLEXT to new table ACDOCT

Once problems (if any) have been resolved, run the program again in update mode. If a large number of records are to be migrated, it is advisable to execute the report in the background. It is also possible to restrict the operation to a set of individual ledgers. If logs are clean, check the allocation settings by running transaction GCA9 as requested at the end of the log. Resolve any inconsistencies as described in the respective messages.

5.8. Migration of Balances

Complete all activities to migrate balances once the "Conversion of Documents and Line Items to the Data Structure" is complete. Perform the following steps, shown in the figure below, in all clients.

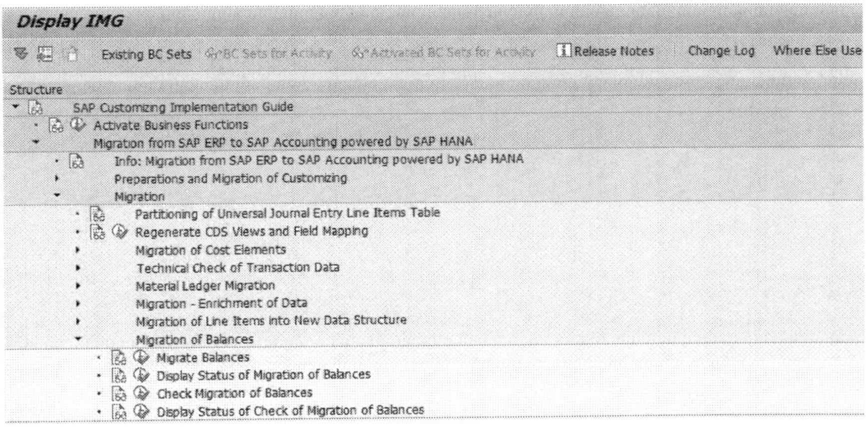
Display IMG
Existing BC Sets
Release Notes
Change Log
Where Else Use
Structure
SAP Customizing Implementation Guide
Activate Business Functions
Migration from SAP ERP to SAP Accounting powered by SAP HANA
Info: Migration from SAP ERP to SAP Accounting powered by SAP HANA
Preparations and Migration of Customizing
Migration
Partitioning of Universal Journal Entry Line Items Table
Regenerate CDS Views and Field Mapping
Migration of Cost Elements
Technical Check of Transaction Data
Material Ledger Migration
Migration - Enrichment of Data
Migration of Line Items into New Data Structure
Migration of Balances
Migrate Balances
Display Status of Migration of Balances
Check Migration of Balances
Display Status of Check of Migration of Balances

Perform all of the below steps, if the source system is using classic Asset Accounting, new Asset Accounting, classic General Ledger Accounting, new General Ledger Accounting, or the SAP Simple Finance add-on 1.0.

5.8.1. 5.8.1 Migrate Balances.

Execute this program so that balances are transferred. If any errors are encountered, resolve them before moving to the next step.

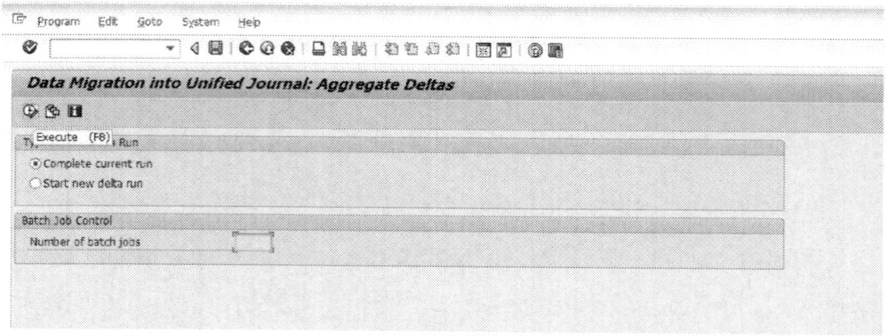
Program
Edit
Goto
System
Help
Data Migration into Unified Journal: Aggregate Deltas
Execute (F8)
Run
Complete current run
Start new delta run
Batch Job Control
Number of batch jobs

5.8.2. Display Status of Balance Conversion

Check the status once the conversion activity is complete. A possible error during the conversion of this activity are those reported on the company codes that are not in scope (e.g. template company codes. In such a case, it may be necessary to delete all existing data for these companies before completing the conversion. SAP will support will be helpful if uncertain how to handle.

T
Message Text
NO FI-GL aggregates for ledger 0L, company code 0001 exist
NO FI-GL aggregates for ledger 0L, company code 0001 exist
LTxt

5.8.3. Check Migration of Balances

Execute this reconciliation step after the conversion of balances for the different applications (FI-GL, CO, FI-AA, and ML) into ACDOCA.

For every former table containing aggregated information, there is a compatibility view that reproduces the original aggregates. This reconciliation step ensures this, i.e. it checks whether there are the same entries with the same values for all fields. As information from different applications is merged, the following deviations from complete agreement apply:

i. If there are inconsistencies between aggregates from different applications, the system ensures complete agreement for FI-GL
ii. The system takes the cost center from CO and does not reconcile with respect to this field in FI
iii. The system takes the amount from ML and does not reconcile with respect to this field in FI
iv. The system does not reconcile the logical system (LOGSYS) in FI
v. When migrating from Classic GL to SAP S/4HANA Finance, the fields ACTIV, KOKRS and AWTYP are not reconciled, if the aggregates cannot be calculated completely from the line items. Reconciliation is not feasible, as these fields did not exist in GLT0, but are now derived.
vi. In case the aggregates from one application are already archived for a given fiscal year, but they are not archived for a different application for the same fiscal year, these values are not shown (for all applications).

5.8.4. Display Status of Check Migration of Balances

Display the status of the conversion of balances. Analyze any errors in detail and correct them before proceeding further. Any errors occurring which cannot be explained and are attributable to system issues should be raised with SAP support.

5.9. Migration: Calculation of Depreciation and Totals Values

As part of the conversion of balances, proceed to build the planned depreciation values for Asset Accounting.

The following prerequisites must be met:

i. Customizing of new Asset Accounting is complete
ii. New Asset Accounting is activated
iii. Transactional data of General Ledger Accounting and Asset Accounting is migrated

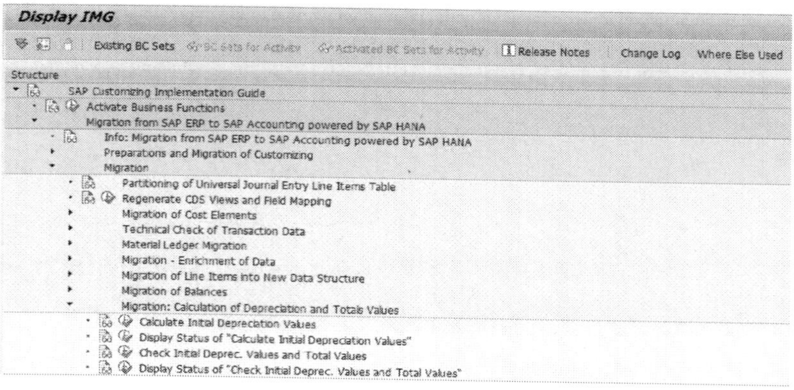
Display IMG
Existing BC Sets
Release Notes
Change Log
Where Else Used
Structure
SAP Customizing Implementation Guide
Activate Business Functions
Migration from SAP ERP to SAP Accounting powered by SAP HANA
Info: Migration from SAP ERP to SAP Accounting powered by SAP HANA
Preparations and Migration of Customizing
Migration
Partitioning of Universal Journal Entry Line Items Table
Regenerate CDS Views and Field Mapping
Migration of Cost Elements
Technical Check of Transaction Data
Material Ledger Migration
Migration - Enrichment of Data
Migration of Line Items into New Data Structure
Migration of Balances
Migration: Calculation of Depreciation and Totals Values
Calculate Initial Depreciation Values
Display Status of "Calculate Initial Depreciation Values"
Check Initial Deprec. Values and Total Values
Display Status of "Check Initial Deprec. Values and Total Values"

5.9.1. Calculate Initial Depreciation Values

Execute this transaction, which is based on the Calculate Depreciation (FAA_DEPRECIATION_CALCULATE) program, to initially build the planned depreciation values for Asset Accounting - i.e. after conversion the transactional data in the previous steps. The program should be run in Test mode first and, if no errors result, executed in update mode.

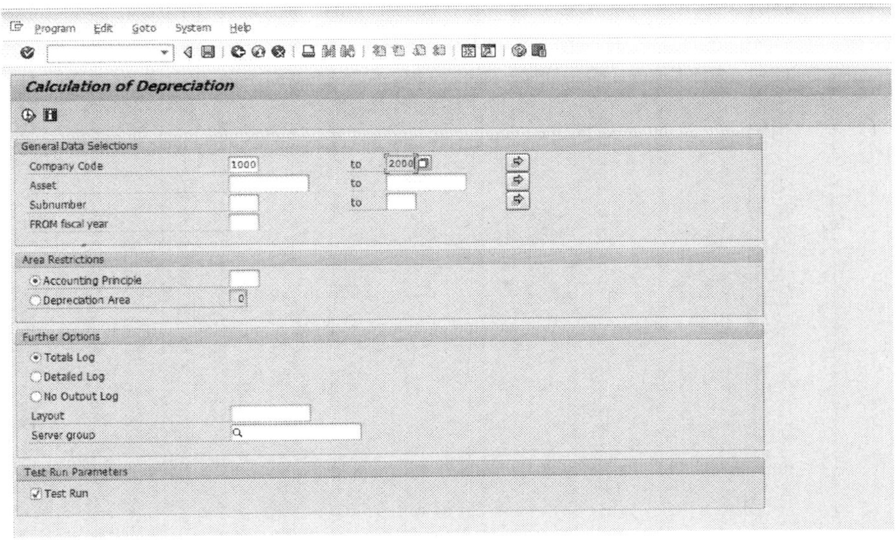
Program Edit Goto System Help
Calculation of Depreciation
General Data Selections
Company Code
1000
to
2000
Asset
to
Subnumber
to
FROM fiscal year
Area Restrictions
Accounting Principle
Depreciation Area
0
Further Options
Totals Log
Detailed Log
No Output Log
Layout
Server group
Test Run Parameters
Test Run

It is possible to defer this activity, for example, if facing difficulty due to time and resource constraints. However, be sure to execute this activity, at the very latest, by the time the first depreciation run takes place.

5.9.2. Display Status of "Calculate Initial Depreciation Values

Display the status for the calculation of initial depreciation values.

5.9.3. Check Initial Depreciation Values and Total Values

Execute this tool to once again reconcile the total values and also the depreciation values.

5.9.4. Display Status of Initial Depreciation Values and Total Values

Display status of the reconciliation activity above. As always, it is important to resolve all inconsistencies before proceeding with the conversion.

5.10. Migration of House Bank Accounts

Unlike previous SAP releases, house banks and bank accounts management in SAP HANA 1610 is managed by SAP Cash Management powered by SAP HANA. This conversion utility helps with the conversion of existing house bank account data to the bank account master data in Bank Account Management (BAM).

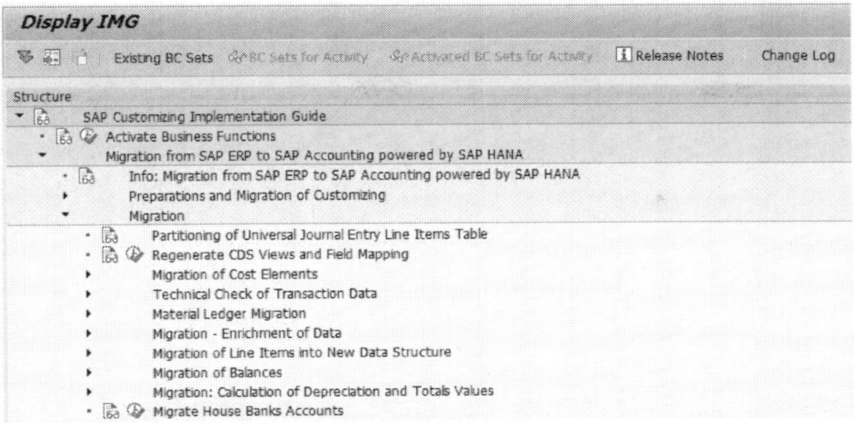
Display IMG
Existing BC Sets
BC Sets for Activity
Activated BC Sets for Activity
Release Notes
Change Log
Structure
SAP Customizing Implementation Guide
Activate Business Functions
Migration from SAP ERP to SAP Accounting powered by SAP HANA
Info: Migration from SAP ERP to SAP Accounting powered by SAP HANA
Preparations and Migration of Customizing
Migration
Partitioning of Universal Journal Entry Line Items Table
Regenerate CDS Views and Field Mapping
Migration of Cost Elements
Technical Check of Transaction Data
Material Ledger Migration
Migration - Enrichment of Data
Migration of Line Items into New Data Structure
Migration of Balances
Migration: Calculation of Depreciation and Totals Values
Migrate House Banks Accounts

Once the list of bank accounts to migrate has been confirmed with business users, utilize this functionality to select which bank accounts to migrate by highlighting them in the list and specifying a data in the "Opened On" field as shown below. To set an account type for multiple house bank accounts, select the house bank account entries, and then choose the Set Account Type button.

Once the program is run, the system generates bank accounts based on selected house bank accounts. Check the conversion status using the status icon displayed at the end of each house bank account entry.

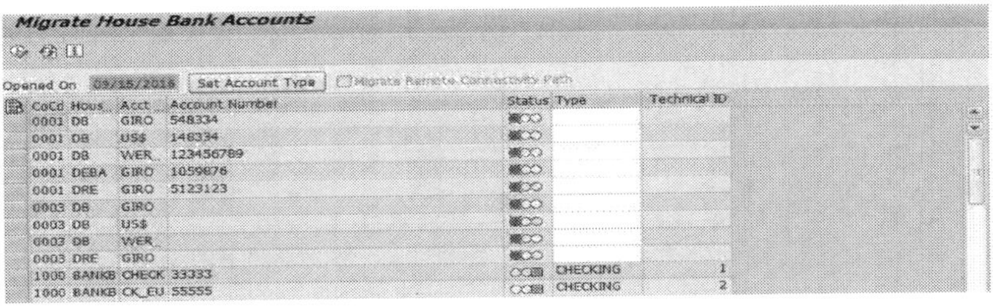
Migrate House Bank Accounts
Opened On
Set Account Type
CoCd
Acct
Account Number
Status
Type
Technical ID
CHECKING
CHECKING

i. Green

This is the desired outcome as house bank account entry is linked to a bank account master record, and the house bank is assigned to the bank account in the master record.

ii. Yellow

The house bank accounts have been migrated to or created in Bank Account Management in an earlier version of SAP Cash Management. The program must be executed again to update the data.

iii. Red

The house bank account entry is not yet linked to a bank account master record. If the status of a house bank account remains red after executing the program, check the conversion log (transaction **SLG1**, specify object **BAM_MIGRATE**) for more information.

5.11. Credit Management Migration

In SAP S/4HANA 1610, the master data from Credit Management in Accounts Receivable (FI-AR), if installed, is migrated to SAP Credit Management in Financial Supply Chain Management (FIN-FSCM-CR).

Execute all the steps in this customizing activity to migrate all relevant data for credit decisions (configuration data, master data, credit exposure data and credit decision data). As a prerequisite, ensure all the steps under the Define Settings for Credit Management Conversion Customizing activity have been executed.

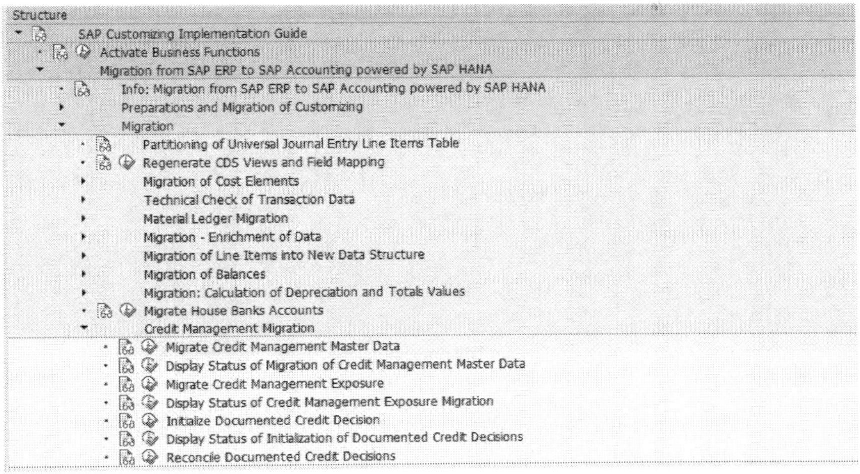
Structure
SAP Customizing Implementation Guide
Activate Business Functions
Migration from SAP ERP to SAP Accounting powered by SAP HANA
Info: Migration from SAP ERP to SAP Accounting powered by SAP HANA
Preparations and Migration of Customizing
Migration
Partitioning of Universal Journal Entry Line Items Table
Regenerate CDS Views and Field Mapping
Migration of Cost Elements
Technical Check of Transaction Data
Material Ledger Migration
Migration - Enrichment of Data
Migration of Line Items into New Data Structure
Migration of Balances
Migration: Calculation of Depreciation and Totals Values
Migrate House Banks Accounts
Credit Management Migration
Migrate Credit Management Master Data
Display Status of Migration of Credit Management Master Data
Migrate Credit Management Exposure
Display Status of Credit Management Exposure Migration
Initialize Documented Credit Decision
Display Status of Initialization of Documented Credit Decisions
Reconcile Documented Credit Decisions

5.11.1. Migrate Credit Management Master Data

Execute this utility so that the business partner role (default: UKM000) will be created for the customer and relevant master data is migrated per customer and credit control area: the credit limits, customer credit groups, credit representative groups, text fields, and risk categories are migrated in accordance with the assignments made in customizing. The relationship UKMSB0 will be created for the respective credit analyst groups.

Note: As a business partner in FIN-FSCM, the customer has only one risk class for all segments. To ensure that the correct risk class is migrated, there must be only one consistent risk category for the customer in all credit control areas.

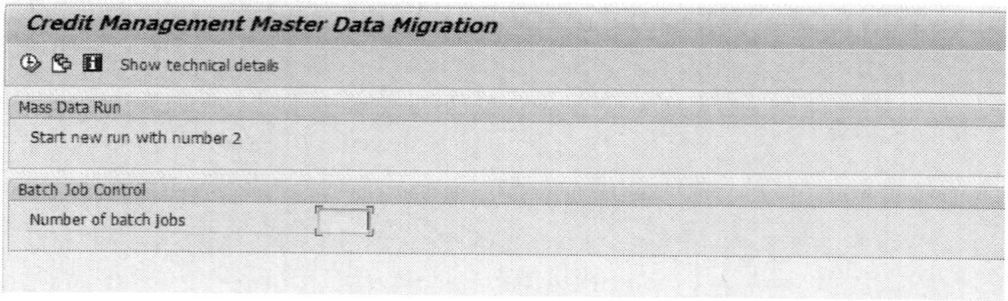
Credit Management Master Data Migration
Show technical details
Mass Data Run
Start new run with number 2
Batch Job Control
Number of batch jobs

5.11.2. Display Status of Migration of Credit Management Master Data

Track the status of conversion of credit management master data.

5.11.3. Migrate Credit Management Exposure

Before migrating credit management exposure for customers, ensure the conversion of credit management master data has been successfully completed. The conversion is executed in two steps:

i. Credit values of open orders and deliveries are migrated to the credit exposure
ii. Payment behavior data from Credit Management is recalculated based on the data in Accounts Receivable (FI-AR)

5.11.4. Display Status of Credit Management Exposure Migration

Execute this utility to display status of credit management exposure conversion.

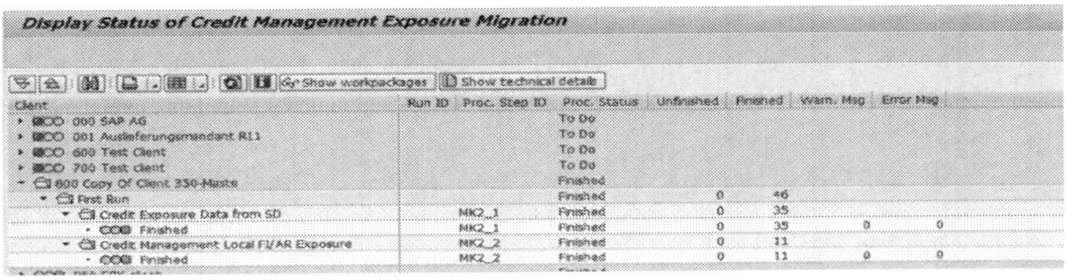
Display Status of Credit Management Exposure Migration
Show workpackages
Show technical details
Client
Run ID
Proc. Step ID
Proc. Status
Unfinished
Finished
Warn. Msg
Error Msg
000 SAP AG
001 Auslieferungsmandant R11
600 Test Client
700 Test client
800 Copy Of Client 350-Maste
First Run
Credit Exposure Data from SD
Finished
Credit Management Local FI/AR Exposure
MK2_1
MK2_2
To Do
Finished

5.11.5. Initialize Documented Credit Decision

Use this activity to initialize documented credit decisions in SAP Credit Management, i.e. sales and delivery documents blocked by credit management. As a prerequisite, ensure the conversion steps for master data and credit management exposure discussed above have completed successfully. Where needed, transaction UKM_CASE can be used to recheck, release or reject blocked documents.

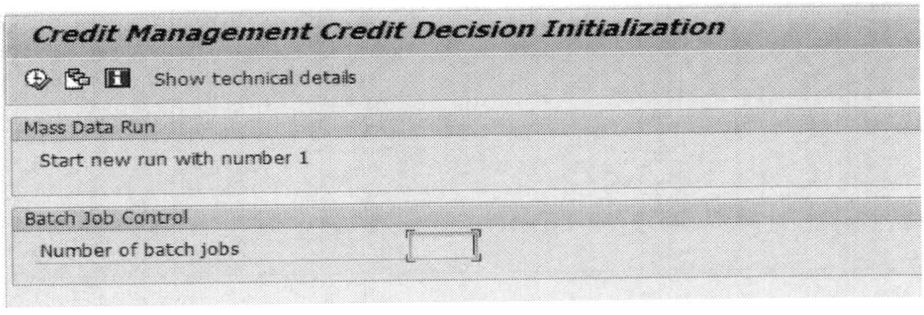
Credit Management Credit Decision Initialization
Show technical details
Mass Data Run
Start new run with number 1
Batch Job Control
Number of batch jobs

5.11.6. Display Status of Initialization of Documented Credit Decisions

Use this activity to display the status of initialization of documented credit decisions.

5.11.7. Reconcile Documented Credit Decisions

Reconcile that for each credit blocked sales and delivery document, a documented credit decision exists.

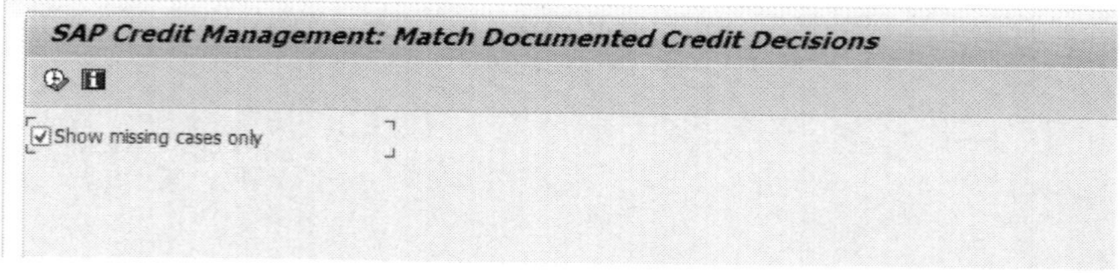
SAP Credit Management: Match Documented Credit Decisions
Show missing cases only

5.12. Verification of Migration Activities with Business Users

As a final step before setting conversion to completed, ensure the comparative analysis between financial data before and after conversion has been carried out. Be sure to include the business users of the organization as these individuals have to sign off on the data as accurate.

The list of transactions that can be used in verifications includes, but is not limited to, the list below. Remember to let business users drive the decision on what needs to be seen to complete this check; the consultant should act as both guide and support to make this happen.

i. Reconcile general ledger 0 with leading ledger 0L (Ledger Comparison transaction GCAC)
ii. The financial statements (program RFBILA00)
iii. The asset history sheet (report RAGITT_ALV01)
iv. The depreciation run for the planned depreciations (program RAHAFA_ALV01)
v. The totals report for cost centers (transaction S_ALR_87013611).
vi. Sales order selection (program RKKBSELL)
vii. The G/L account balances (program RFSSLD00).
viii. General ledger line items (program RFSOPO00)
ix. The compact document journal (program RFBELJ00)
x. Vendor sales (program RFKUML00)
xi. The vendor open item list (program RFKOPO00)
xii. Customer sales (program RFKUML00)
xiii. The customer open item list (program RFKOPO00)
xiv. Customer recurring entry original documents (program RFDAUB00)

5.13. Set Migration to completed

After successfully reconciling the before and after transactional data and balances, the conversion can be deemed to have completed successfully. Follow the customizing path below to set the indicator conversion completed. **Note: This indicator must be set only if all errors of conversion are corrected.**

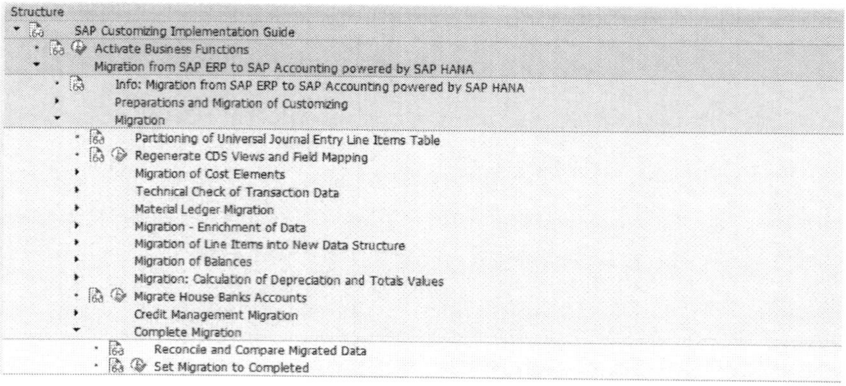
Structure
SAP Customizing Implementation Guide
Activate Business Functions
Migration from SAP ERP to SAP Accounting powered by SAP HANA
Info: Migration from SAP ERP to SAP Accounting powered by SAP HANA
Preparations and Migration of Customizing
Migration
Partitioning of Universal Journal Entry Line Items Table
Regenerate CDS Views and Field Mapping
Migration of Cost Elements
Technical Check of Transaction Data
Material Ledger Migration
Migration - Enrichment of Data
Migration of Line Items into New Data Structure
Migration of Balances
Migration: Calculation of Depreciation and Totals Values
Migrate House Banks Accounts
Credit Management Migration
Complete Migration
Reconcile and Compare Migrated Data
Set Migration to Completed

After this step is done, users are able to make postings in the system again. Otherwise users continue to receive the message defined earlier in the Customizing activity "Define Message Types for Posting Before and During Conversion."

6. Post Conversion Customization

Perform the following post conversion customization activities once all the conversion activities are complete.

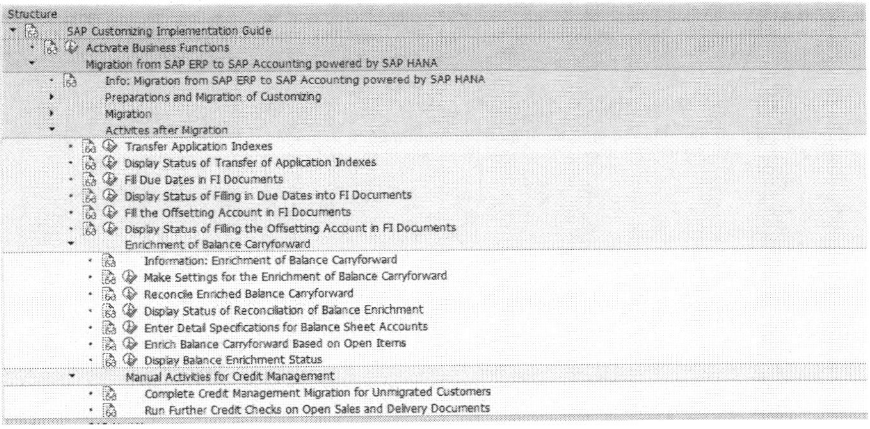
Structure
SAP Customizing Implementation Guide
Activate Business Functions
Migration from SAP ERP to SAP Accounting powered by SAP HANA
Info: Migration from SAP ERP to SAP Accounting powered by SAP HANA
Preparations and Migration of Customizing
Migration
Activities after Migration
Transfer Application Indexes
Display Status of Transfer of Application Indexes
Fill Due Dates in FI Documents
Display Status of Filling in Due Dates into FI Documents
Fill the Offsetting Account in FI Documents
Display Status of Filling the Offsetting Account in FI Documents
Enrichment of Balance Carryforward
Information: Enrichment of Balance Carryforward
Make Settings for the Enrichment of Balance Carryforward
Reconcile Enriched Balance Carryforward
Display Status of Reconciliation of Balance Enrichment
Enter Detail Specifications for Balance Sheet Accounts
Enrich Balance Carryforward Based on Open Items
Display Balance Enrichment Status
Manual Activities for Credit Management
Complete Credit Management Migration for Unmigrated Customers
Run Further Credit Checks on Open Sales and Delivery Documents

6.1. Transfer Application Indexes

If Data Aging is active (DAAG_DATA_AGING is activated) in the system, start moving the indexes in the "cold" area of the database using transaction FINS_MIG_INIT_COLD. This step transfers application indexes to the database cold area in order to reduce main memory consumption.

When the financial accounting documents were archived, it was possible to keep the application indexes (that is, BSIS, BSAS, BSID, BSAD, BSIK, and BSAK) in the database. Data aging is a new concept available with the HANA database and replaces the old archiving concept. It allows aging data to be moved to the "cold area" of the database from the "hot area," where data can be instantly accessed.

In S/4HANA Finance, the application indexes that correspond to non-archived documents are calculated on the basis of the financial accounting document. The application indexes that correspond to already archived documents are stored in tables (that is, the tables BSIS_BCK, BSAS_BCK, BSID_BCK, BSAD_BCK, BSIK_BCK, and BSAK_BCK) in the cold area of the database. This program transfers these entries into the cold area of the database.

6.2. Display Status of Transfer of Application Indexes

Execute this utility to display the status of the transfer of application indexes to the database cold area.

6.3. Fill Due Dates in FI Documents

Use this customizing activity to fill the new due date fields in the FI line items for customers and vendors and for G/L account line items that have a base line date.

6.4. Display Status of Filling in Due Dates into FI Documents

Display the status of filling in the due dates into FI documents (transaction FINS_MIG_MONITOR_DUE).

6.5. Fill the Offsetting Account in FI Documents

Once the due dates are filled without any errors, proceed with filling the offsetting account in FI documents (transaction FINS_MIG_GKONT). Before running this utility, ensure the customizing activity to define the offsetting account determination type has been completed.

6.6. Display Status of Filling the Offsetting Account in FI Documents

After filling the offsetting account in FI documents, check the result or status using transaction FINS_MIG_MONITOR_GKO.

7. Other Requirements for Conversion

7.1. System Prerequisites

7.1.1. Confirm Unicode Compliance

Note that any path to a target system based on SAP NetWeaver 7.51 (such as S/4HANA 1610) requires the source system to already be on Unicode, as described in SAP Note 2171334. If the source system is a non-Unicode system, plan and prepare the conversion of non-Unicode source systems.

- Only Unicode systems are supported on SAP S/4 HANA 1610
- Standalone Unicode conversion procedure similar to system copy is offered by software provisioning manager
- The conversion to Unicode system with NetWeaver 7.4 or older release can optionally be combined with other procedures (update, conversion, or DMO), but requires preparatory activities (including consistency check, clean-up obsolete data, and transformation of custom code).
- With non-Unicode source system, shadow system would also have to be non-Unicode (which is not supported on 7.5). Note that any path to a target system based on SAP NetWeaver 7.50 (such as SAP ERP 6.0 EHP 8) requires the source system to already be on Unicode, as described in SAP Note 2171334

Unicode Conversion reparation steps

- Check restrictions and SAP notes – 548016, 540911, 2108396, 765475
- Check SAP Basis and functional requirements – SAP Frontend, HR functionality, SAP Office, CRM Business Transaction and Content server
- Perform consistency check for cluster cables
- Make ABAP programs Unicode-compliant – transaction UCCHECK
- Convert customer code pages to Unicode-based code page structure
- Delete Matchcode IDs
- Data Maintenance - Reducing Data Volume, Archive Obsolete Data of Tables
- Pre-conversion with SPUMG during system uptime -- the Database Migration Option (DMO) uses the result of SPUMG

7.1.2. Verify Single Stack

The source system has to be an AS ABAP only system. Dual-stack systems (AS ABAP and AS Java combined in one system) are not supported for the conversion. If the system is dual-stack, split it prior to the conversion.

Dual-stack split procedure is offered by Software Provisioning Manager 1.0 (integrated as of SL Toolset 1.0 SPS09, no longer offered standalone).

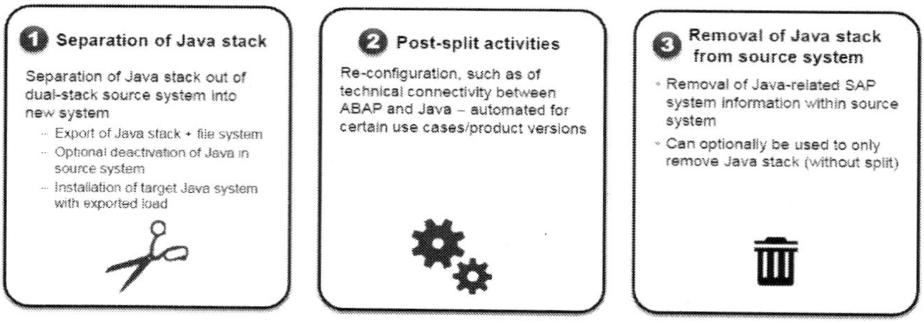
1 Separation of Java stack
Separation of Java stack out of dual-stack source system into new system
– Export of Java stack + file system
– Optional deactivation of Java in source system
– Installation of target Java system with exported load
2 Post-split activities
Re-configuration, such as of technical connectivity between ABAP and Java – automated for certain use cases/product versions
3 Removal of Java stack from source system
• Removal of Java-related SAP system information within source system
• Can optionally be used to only remove Java stack (without split)

7.2. Productive Sizing

For productive (brownfield) sizing, there are two different approaches possible. The first approach is more straightforward and can be applied as a first rough assessment, while the second approach (report) is much more detailed and therefore also more reliable. Both approaches should be considered complementary, the first as a rough assessment and the second as the more reliable and certainly preferable one.

i. Simple approach

To get a first ballpark estimate of the required HANA Main Memory, first check the size of the current database using the standard SAP monitoring tools. This assumes is that the source system is well-maintained and uncompressed. The recommendation from SAP is to take half the size of the disk-based database, include a safety buffer of 20%, and add 50 GB fixed size for code, stack and other services. This means, if the database is currently approximately 2000 GB in size (tables plus indexes), the maximum memory consumption will be 1250 GB (2000 GB/2 * 1,2 + 50 GB).

Also, consider estimated future data growth in planning. SAP doesn't expect changes in memory requirements for applications using liveCache. If using SAP HANA Enterprise Search, add 20% extra memory resources.

ii. Estimation

To estimate the HANA CPU requirements, first identify the CPU consumption of the database. For example, look at the CPU consumption of the database processes using SAP's monitoring tools. To fully support the parallel processing capabilities of HANA, SAP prefers 3X more CPU power for HANA than for disk based databases without parallelization. This also considers the load for running OLTP and reporting simultaneously and includes a moderate use of SAP HANA Enterprise Search. Extensive usage of SAP HANA Enterprise Search capabilities may require additional CPU resources.

To give a prediction regarding the required HANA disk space (or total net disk space), consider the net data size on disk (anyDB) and the disk space required for delta merges. During a delta merge, the affected tables are temporarily duplicated on disk for a short period of time. The disk space for merges is calculated by taking the sum of the two biggest tables and including this value into the calculation. Finally, add 25GB for the space required by the statistics server, HANA metadata, etc.

The final calculation looks as follows:

HANA disk space (Total Net Disk Space) =

*(Net Data Size anyDB + Disk Space for Merges) / 4 (compression) * 1,2 (20% safety buffer) + 25GB*

If using SAP HANA Enterprise Search, add 20% extra disk resources.

More information regarding SAP HANA storage requirements can be found in this document: (https://www.sap.com/documents/2015/03/74cdb554-5a7c-0010-82c7-eda71af511fa.html). Note that SAP doesn't expect any changes concerning CPU, memory and network requirements for the ABAP application server. This means that the existing hardware and network infrastructure can still be used.

iii. Sizing Report

Refer to SAP Note 1872170 (Suite on HANA and S/4 HANA sizing report) if performing HANA memory sizing of an already productive system. This SAP Note implements a program to estimate the memory space requirement for the database tables of Suite on

HANA systems. The program runs on non-HANA systems and is the preferred choice to size an already productive system.

7.3. Maintenance Planner checks

Use of Maintenance Planner is mandatory for conversion to S/4 HANA 1610. Maintenance Planner is a solution hosted by SAP and offers easy maintenance of systems in your landscape. The Maintenance Planner checks the system with regards to business functions, industry solutions, and add-ons. If there is no valid path for the conversion (for example, the add-on is not released yet), the Maintenance Planner prevents the conversion. The Maintenance Planner helps to download files (add-ons, packages, DBDs, Stack File – the input for SUM) that the Software Update Manager (SUM) uses to convert to SAP S/4HANA. For more information regarding Maintenance Planner see SAP Help

Besides the general preparations in the Maintenance Planner, the following preparatory steps are required to use Maintenance Planner.

i. Update SPAM/SAINT to at least patch 62
ii. Apply SAP note 2186164 to SAP Solution Manager system
iii. Create RFC destination SM_<SID>CLNT<CLNT>_READ in the Solution Manager to client 000 of upgrade source system.

7.3.1. Always-on and Always-Off Business Functions

In SAP S/4HANA on-premise edition, business functions can have the following status: always-on, customer-switchable, and always-off. This results in the following behavior during the conversion:

- If a business function was switched on in the start release system, but defined as always off in SAP S/4HANA, on-premise edition, then a system conversion is not yet possible with this release at the current point in time.
  (SAP 2240359 - SAP S/4HANA, Always-Off Business Functions)
- If a business function was switched off in the start release system, but defined as always on in the target release, then the business function will be automatically activated during the conversion. (SAP Note 2240360 - SAP S/4HANA, Always-On Business Functions).

7.3.2. Industry Solutions

SAP S/4HANA, on-premise edition 1610 supports the following industries (SAP Note 2333141):

i. Consumer Products,
ii. Wholesale,
iii. Life Sciences,
iv. Aerospace & Defense (A&D),
v. High-tech,

vi. Industrial Machinery & Components (IM&C),
vii. Automotive
viii. Chemicals
ix. Mining
x. Mill Products
xi. Utilities
xii. Banking
xiii. Insurance
xiv. Public Sector
xv. Engineering
xvi. Construction & Operations (EC&O)
xvii. Professional Services
xviii. Telecommunication
xix. Sports & Entertainment
xx. Transportation & Logistics
xxi. Contract Accounts Receivable and Payable (FI-CA)
xxii. Higher Education and Research
xxiii. Defense and Security
xxiv. Oil and Gas
xxv. Retail

7.3.3. Add-ons

Check whether the add-on supplier has released the specific add-on for usage with the installation SAP S/4HANA. If add-on is not supported in S/4HANA 1610, delete it before SUM tool starts. An unsupported add-on will cause a critical issue during SUM conversion.

i. SAP S/4HANA, on-premise edition 1610 'Standard' add-ons: The release information is provided in the SAP note 2214409 and in the feature scope description for S/4HANA, on-premise edition 1610 product version.

ii. SAP S/4HANA, on-premise edition 1610 '(Standard) Custom Development' add-ons: For a solution categorized as '(Standard), Custom Development' for the SAP S/4HANA, on-premise edition 1610 system, please contact SAP Custom Development at least three months before implementing SAP S/4HANA, because sufficient time might be required in case of adjustments.

iii. Partner add-ons: Information on released partner add-ons are not part of this note and can be found in SAP Note 2392527. If 3rd-party Add-ons are installed in the system which is not yet supported on S/4HANA, refer to the SAP Note 2308014, which describes the steps to proceed to S/4HANA in this scenario.

iv. Uninstalling ABAP add-ons: Information on uninstalling ABAP Add-ons can be found in SAP Note 2011192.

In searching for an add-on that is neither in the list above nor in the related notes, please contact SAP Support (under XX-SER-REL) or the specific partner for non-SAP Products.

7.4. SAP Fiori Front-End Server

SAP Solutions use the Fiori User Experience (UX) to provide a personalized, responsive, simple, comprehensive user experience. It can be used across all device types. Fiori apps provide access to the most recent version of back end data using OData services. Using previously defined roles, it is possible to specify which apps and data a user is allowed to access. The following are the deployment options:

i. **Central Hub Deployment option** the front-end components with user interface (UI) layer are separated from back-end components that contain the business logic and back-end data. This provides strategic advantages of decoupling the lifecycle of UI apps from backend systems and allows single point of maintenance of UI.

ii. **Embedded Deployment Option** Front-end server and back-end servers are installed in the same server. It is not recommended for a production environment.

7.5. Development steps related to custom code and fields

7.5.1. Check custom code and modifications

The conversion to SAP Accounting powered by SAP HANA generates new data structures in Accounting and replaces existing tables with same-named views. Perform the following checks and activities in the test system:

i. For write accesses to the tables in the customer objects in the customer namespace, replace these accesses, since the views with same names allow only read access.

ii. For customer-specific views in current objects in the customer namespace for the tables that no longer exist, replace these views with an open-SQL SELECT or the call of a read module, since the data dictionary does not support database views that are based on other views.

iii. If migrating from classic Asset Accounting, note that batch input programs for AB01 are no longer supported in new Asset Accounting. If using customer-defined programs, you must convert these to BAPIs.

Please refer to SAP Note 1976487 (Information about adjusting customer-specific programs to the simplified data model for SAP S/4HANA Finance 1610) for additional details on how to deal with customer specific code.

7.5.2. Perform FI Custom Code Checks

Analyze the system for Custom Objects impacted by the simplified data model in S/4HANA Finance. The majority of custom code will be unaffected by changes to the underlying tables as a result of CDS views replacing the old tables. Review the following areas where remediation action will be needed. (Note: Write accesses to standard SAP tables are not recommended, but if they exist, modify them as described below)

i. **Write access to totals tables and index tables in FI and CO**: Remove all write accesses to these objects from source code (operations INSERT, UPDATE, DELETE, and MODIFY). These totals tables, e.g. FAGLFLEXT, COSS, have been replaced by views.

ii. **Read accesses to totals tables and index tables in FI and CO**: Remove keyword "ORDER BY PRIMARY KEY" from SELECTs from views with the same name to avoid syntax errors. Replace this with an explicit field list, for example, ORDER BY BUKRS HKONT AUGDT AUGBL ZUONR GJAHR BELNR BUZEI

iii. **Views for totals tables and index tables**: Remove all views based on the old database tables. The ABAP Dictionary does not support database views based on other views.

iv. **Write accesses to the line item tables**: FAGLFLEXA, FMGLFLEXA, PSGLFLEXA, JVGLFLEXA, and ZZ<CUST>A must be converted to the table ACDOCA.

v. **COEP**: Use the new ABAP class CL_FCO_COEP_UPDATE for all write accesses to COEP outside the software component SAP_FIN.

vi. **Asset Accounting**: Remove write accesses to the tables ANEA, ANEP, ANEK, ANLC, ANLP without replacing them.

vii. **Material Ledger**: Remove write accesses to the ML document tables (MLHD, MLIT, MLPP, MLCR, MLCD) if previously changing documents of the transaction type "UP" ("Update"). Write accesses for other transaction types are still possible.

viii. **T012K/T012T**: Convert write accesses to the tables T012T and T012K, to the tables FCLM_BAM_AMD, FCLM_BAM_AMD_CUR, FCLM_BAM_AMT_T, and FCLM_BAM_ACLINK2.

For aadditional details you can refer SAP Note 1976487.

7.5.3. Perform Credit Management Custom Code Checks

Analyze the system for custom objects impacted by updates to SAP objects in the SAP HANA simplifications list. It is important to adopt these customer objects to the data model changes in FI and SD Credit Management. Details are provided in SAP Notes 2227014 and 2217124

7.5.4. Perform SD Custom Code Checks

Analyze the system for custom objects impacted by updates to SD objects in the SAP HANA simplifications list. It is important to adopt these customer objects to the data model changes in the SD Module. The SAP objects impacted by changes comprise the following:

i. Sales Document status tables i.e. VBUK and VBUP
ii. Sales Document Partner i.e. VBPA
iii. Sales Index e.g. VAKPA, VAPMA, etc.
iv. SD Pricing i.e. KONV
v. SD Rebate Processing i.e. VBOX

Additional details are provided in SAP Notes 2198647, 2220005 and 2200691.

7.5.5. Perform MM Custom Code Checks

The main MM data model change is the introduction of the Table MATDOC, which replaces data stored in MKPF, MSEG and some other tables. Perform the following activities as required:

i. Add customer include CI_COBL to NSDM_S_ITEM: This is a preparatory step for conversion of material transactional data to MATDOC. Additional details are available in SAP Note 2240878.
ii. If there write accesses to those tables MKPF and MSEG or customer APPEND or INCLUDES in the these objects, then adapt these customer objects to the data model changes in the MM Module as described in SAP Notes 2206980 and 2194618.

The full list of tables impacted by the introduction of MATDOC can be seen in SAP Note 2206980. Most existing objects will remain unaffected by the changes as there are CDS Views providing on-the-fly access to the information in MKPF, MSEG, etc. based on

MATDOC. However, if there write accesses to those tables, or customer APPEND or INCLUDES in the old objects, then remediation is required, as described above.

Note that in MATDOC the aggregated actual stock quantities will not be persisted any more in the hybrid or replaced aggregation tables. Instead, actual stock quantity data will be calculated on the fly from the new material document table MATDOC, for which some of those additional special fields are used. Hence, with the new MM-IM data model, the system will work on database level in an INSERT only mode without DB locks. Nevertheless, for stock decreasing processes, there will be still ABAP locks to ensure stock consistency. A further advantage of the new MM-IM data model is the capability of simple and fast reporting because the most information is all in one place -- MATDOC.

7.5.6. Perform MM Classification System Custom Code Checks

Analyze the system for custom objects impacted by updates to MM Classification System objects in the SAP HANA simplifications list. It is important to adopt these customer objects to the data model changes in the MM Module. The SAP objects impacted by changes comprise the following:

iii. Classification domain field length extensions: Enhancement of the classification domain came from the enhancement of the material number; refer to SAP Note 2221293. The enhanced domains from the classification system are: CUOBN, ATWRT, ATSCH, ATWTB.

Details are available in SAP Note 2221293.

7.5.7. Perform EHSM Custom Code Checks

Analyze the system for custom objects impacted by updates to EHS in the SAP HANA simplifications list. It is important to adopt these customer objects to the data model changes in EHSM Module. The areas impacted by changes comprise the following:

i. Analytical reporting for EHS using SAP Netweaver Business Intelligence (BI)

ii. Data extraction into SAP Netweaver Business Intelligence (BI) for risks, chemicals and incidents

iii. Incident Management (EHS-MGM-INC) and Risk Assessment (EHS-MGM-RAS) functions

iv. Industrial Hygiene and Safety (EHS-IHS) and SAP Environmental Compliance (EC) interfaces

Details are provided in SAP Notes 2217208, 2217206 and 2241080.

7.5.8. Perform PP Custom Code Checks

The original planning files MDVM/MDVL and DBVM/DBVL no longer exist and have been replaced by the new planning file PPH_DBVM. If existing custom code only reads from the tables DBVM or DBVL, no adaption is necessary. Queries from table DBVM or DBVL will be redirected to the new planning file PPH_DBVM by compatibility views

If existing custom code creates planning file entries directly by updating or inserting into tables MDVM, MDVL, DBVM, or DBVL, then adapt the custom code and call function module DISPSATZ_ERSTELLEN instead.

Custom code reading one of the tables RQIT, RQHD, or MDRI will no longer work. Read table RESB instead.

Additional details are provided in SAP Notes 2227059 and 2229126

7.5.9. Handling Customer-Defined Fields and Interfaces

Customer defined fields, similar to custom code, are impacted by the S/4HANA Finance 1610 conversion process. If using new General Ledger Accounting and also using customer-defined fields, these fields are generated to the appropriate compatibility views.

For customer fields in BSEG and the index tables, note the following for the creation of the views with the same names:

i. If a customer field exists in both BSEG and in the indexes, it is automatically generated into the view with the same name. It is not transferred into a view with the same name if the customer field only exists in the index. In this case the field must first be included in the BSEG table and filled using a customer program.

ii. If transferring data from Z tables to new General Ledger Accounting during the conversion, delete the data of these Z tables before the conversion to SAP S/4HANA 1610. If the data is not deleted, the data of the Z tables is migrated again and transferred to the new table structure. The values would then be duplicated.

iii. If using interfaces to connect the system to external systems that make postings to General Ledger Accounting (in real time or subsequently), check whether adjustments need to be made to the interfaces.

iv. In the SAP S/4HANA 1610, ALE scenarios are only partially supported. The migrated S/4HANA system cannot serve as an ALE receiver for CO line items. The reason is that FI and CO line items use the same persistence table in S/4HANA 1610. Therefore, the CO line items cannot be posted alone without the FI line items they belong to. SAP does not provide a check to determine if this scenario is used in the system. Carry out this check manually. ALE scenarios for the distribution of CO master data, such as cost centers, continue to be supported.

7.5.10. Import check reports into the system

Perform the below steps before installing SAP S/4HANA 1610. Perform these steps both in Customizing system (i.e. development) and in any downstream systems (e.g. quality, pre-production, production, etc.).

Performing the conversion for Asset Accounting is not possible unless source system was migrated to new General Ledger Accounting.

Process overview:

i. *Check prerequisite for using new Asset Accounting - refer to SAP Note 2333236 for more details*
ii. *Lock users*
iii. *Perform period-end closing*
iv. *Perform a backup*
v. *Install the SAP S/4HANA Finance 1610*
vi. *Migrate to New General Ledger Accounting*

If using the classic General Ledger Accounting until now, the system will be migrated automatically to the new General Ledger Accounting.

7.6. Additional Information for Migrating from Classic General Ledger

7.6.1. New GL Functionality

There are additional restrictions on functional scope to consider when migrating from a Classic General Ledger financial system. Unlike the earlier strategies for conversion to the New General Ledger Accounting, the following implementation scenarios are not supported for conversion to S/4 HANA Finance:

i. Document splitting and therefore the creation of the balance sheet on other dimensions, e.g. profit center, segment.
ii. Ledger approach for parallel accounting – i.e. replacement of parallel accounts: parallel ledgers will not be added as part of the conversion, but can be implemented post-conversion.
iii. Conversion from Special Purpose Ledger to new General Ledger Accounting.

To enable these functionalities of the New GL entails a separate implementation project to be carried out before attempting conversion to S/4HANA Finance 1610.

7.6.2. Profit Center Accounting in Classic General Ledger

Consider the following restrictions when migrating from the existing Profit Center Accounting (PCA) solution in classic GL:

i. If using PCA for profit and loss accounts, conversion to PCA in the Universal Journal is possible. Since Profit Center is one of the characteristics.

ii. If using PCA for balance sheet accounts, converting to PCA in the Universal Journal is not possible.

iii. Where currencies used in PCA differ from those in the General Ledger, those additional currencies must be added as parallel currencies in SAP HANA 1610 (additional information is available in SAP Note 39919).

iv. Local PCA documents, i.e. those that are entered using special posting transactions, are not transferable to SAP HANA. This will result in differences for the reconciliation between Profit Center Accounting and classic General Ledger Accounting.

7.6.3. Preparations for Migrating Cost of Sales Accounting.

After conversion, the necessary data for carrying out Cost of Sales accounting can be stored in the universal journal, i.e. it is no longer necessary to maintain a COS accounting Ledger.

Unlike classic General Ledger Accounting, the system determines the functional area in new General Ledger Accounting as soon as documents are entered. This changes the timing of the substitution of the functional area, from event 0005 to event 0006. More information about the derivation of the functional area is available in SAP Note 740519

7.6.4. Considerations for Foreign Currency Valuation

If foreign currency valuation is being utilized in the existing system, reset all valuations using transaction SAPF100 (using the Valuation for Balance Sheet Preparation). This ensures that the valuation differences in the open items are set to zero.

Note that SAPF100 is no longer supported in S/4HANA Finance, and incorrect values might be the result of not initializing the valuation differences before conversion.

If valuation areas are not currently being used, switch to using valuation areas and accounts dependent on valuation areas to ensure the correct application of fully automatic foreign currency valuation with parallel accounts.

7.7. Migrating to S/4HANA 1610 System

7.7.1. Selecting a Pre-configuration mode

If choosing single system mode, these actions take place during downtime in the Downtime roadmap step of SUM. If choosing standard or advanced mode, continue to use the SAP system in productive operation during these actions, as they run in the Preprocessing roadmap step of SUM.

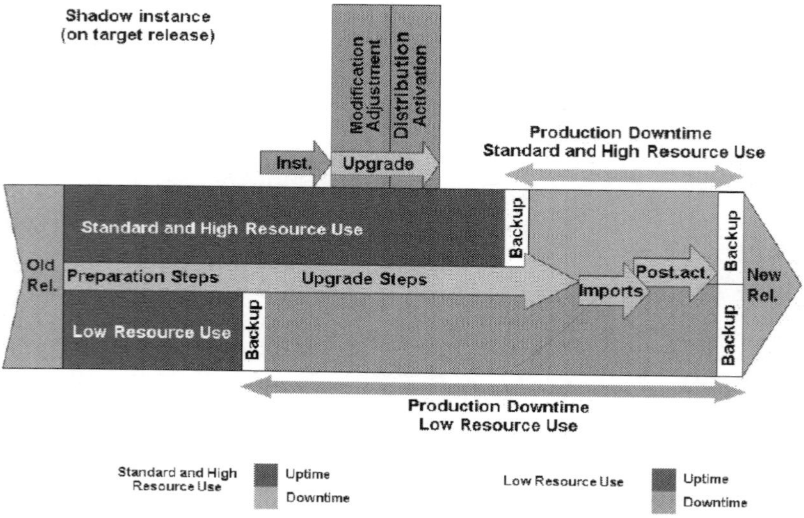
Shadow instance
(on target release)
Modification
Adjustment
Distribution
Activation
Inst.
Upgrade
Production Downtime
Standard and High Resource Use
Standard and High Resource Use
Backup
Old
Rel.
Preparation Steps
Upgrade Steps
Imports
Post.act.
Backup
New
Rel.
Low Resource Use
Backup
Backup
Production Downtime
Low Resource Use
Standard and High
Resource Use
Uptime
Downtime
Low Resource Use
Uptime
Downtime

Pre-configuration Mode	**Features**	**Scenario**
Single System	• Early start of downtime. • Longer downtime • Shadow instance stops original instance and runs exclusively	• Low system resources • Newly installed system • Updates with a focus on the overall update processing time instead of the downtime only
Standard	• Standard downtime optimization. • Late start of downtime – import and shadow system operation while the SAP system is still in productive operation	• Standard system resources available
Advanced	• Extensive downtime optimization • Higher complexity	• High system resources available • Maximum possible downtime optimization depending on the target release and SUM version

Recommendations for Choosing the Pre-configuration Mode

Depending on the situation, choose the pre-configuration mode that best meets requirements. Here are some recommendations:

i. If migrating a sandbox system, the system downtime might not be important. Choosing the pre-configuration mode single system may be the most appropriate. Using this pre-configuration mode, the prompt to start the downtime appears early compared to the standard and advanced pre-configuration modes. Since this is the last user interaction for a longer time, this allows the update procedure run unattended (for example, during the weekend).

ii. If migrating a production system, the impact on productive operation must be considered. If choosing the standard or advanced pre-configuration mode, the shadow system is operated during uptime. This means that the source release system and the shadow system compete for the system resources. If the resource usage is of concern for the system, it makes sense to choose the pre-configuration mode standard since this mode uses only a limited amount of system resources.

iii. If migrating a production system with a high demand for minimal downtime, the impact of the running shadow system on the source release system might not be important. In this case, it could make sense to choose advanced to shorten the overall runtime as much as possible.

7.7.2. System Switch migration procedure

This procedure installs an instance of the target release, the shadow system, in parallel with the current source release system in the same database. The parallel system contains all the software of the target release and is used to perform actions on the target release while the source release is still in productive operation.

Operating two instances in parallel places increased demands on free space in the file system, in the database, and on the system resources. No precise guidelines can be given for the duration of a conversion. The duration of the shadow system installation depends to a great extent on the amount of data, the database system, and the hardware and can take several hours. Although the system can still be used in productive operation, take into account a possible performance decrease during this shadow system installation process. If necessary, some parameters in the production system might need to be adjusted to allow operating the production and the shadow systems in parallel. The following figure shows the process flow of the conversion with the major steps of the process.

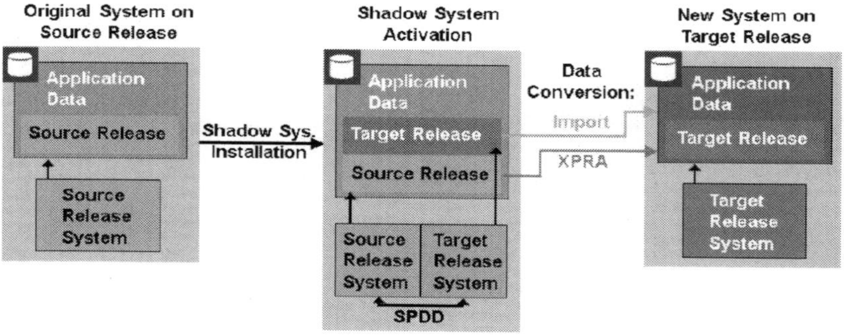
Original System on Source Release
Application Data
Source Release
Source Release System
Shadow Sys. Installation
Shadow System Activation
Application Data
Target Release
Source Release
Source Release System
Target Release System
SPDD
Data Conversion:
Import
XPRA
New System on Target Release
Application Data
Target Release
Target Release System

During the SAP system upgrade if an additional host is available then run the shadow instance on remote host so that there's no impact on the Production activities during uptime. Below are the configurations and input needed during the Configuration Phase of SUM tool to enable shadow instance to run on Remote host.

i. Identify the host
ii. In the configuration Phase of SUM tool provide the host name for Remote Shadow instance

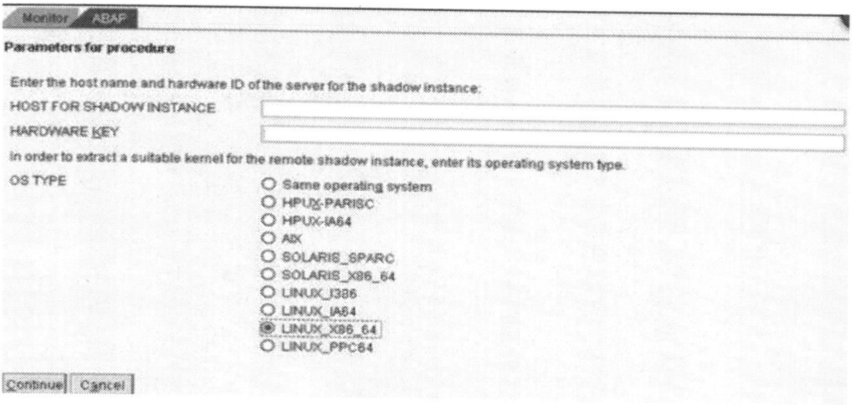
Monitor
ABAP
Parameters for procedure
Enter the host name and hardware ID of the server for the shadow instance:
HOST FOR SHADOW INSTANCE
HARDWARE KEY
In order to extract a suitable kernel for the remote shadow instance, enter its operating system type.
OS TYPE
Same operating system
HPUX-PARISC
HPUX-IA64
AIX
SOLARIS_SPARC
SOLARIS_X86_64
LINUX_I386
LINUX_IA64
LINUX_X86_64
LINUX_PPC64
Continue
Cancel

iii. Prepare the User environment (SIDADM and DBSID) by using SWPM Lifecycle options.

iv. In the configuration Phase also provide the OS of the target for Remote Shadow host

v. Obtain the hardware key by executing SAPLICENSE -get provided SAP kernel is on the host. Else, copy the SAP exe directory and get the HARDWARE Key to be keyed in

vi. Copy the SSFS key generated on CI and place the same place holder for shadow instance.

vii. /usr/sap/<SID>/SYS/global/security/rsecssfs/key

viii. /usr/sap/<SID>/SYS/global/security/rsecssfs/data

ix. Start and stop the Shadow instance as per SUM tool recommendations during various phases manually on Remote host.

The above steps will enable the shadow instance run smoothly on remote host and achieve target to speed up upgrade, with no interruption to production activities during uptime (and thereby reduce downtime).

7.8. Important OSS notes

2346431 - SAP S/4HANA 1610: Release Information Note

2333141 - SAP S/4HANA 1610: Restriction Note

2392527 - SAP S/4HANA, on-premise edition 1610: Compatible partner products

2356208 - SAP S/4HANA "SAP FIORI FOR SAP S/4HANA 1610": Release Information

2241080 - Custom code check content for SAP S/4HANA.

2377310 - Add. info. on converting to SAP S/4 HANA using SUM SP20

References

1. SAP S/4 HANA migration related blogs written by partners and SAP SMEs
2. S/4 HANA SAP Notes referred during migration
3. Series of SAP S/4 HANA Press books released in last two years
4. SAP authorized training received in last three years

Disclaimer

90016417R00104

Made in the USA
Columbia, SC
24 February 2018